WeightWatchers®

Fabulous recipes for evening meals

Satisfying Suppers

First published in Great Britain by Simon & Schuster UK Ltd, 2013
A CBS Company

Copyright © 2013, Weight Watchers International, Inc.
Simon & Schuster Illustrated Books, Simon & Schuster UK Ltd,
First Floor, 222 Gray's Inn Road, London WC1X 8HB

www.simonandschuster.co.uk

Simon & Schuster Australia, Sydney
Simon & Schuster India, New Delhi

Weight Watchers, **ProPoints** and the **ProPoints** icon are the registered
trademarks of Weight Watchers International Inc and are used under license
by Weight Watchers (UK) Ltd.

Weight Watchers Publications: Jane Griffiths, Linda Palmer and Nina McKerlie.

Recipes written by: Sue Ashworth, Sue Beveridge, Tamsin Burnett-Hall,
Cas Clarke, Siân Davies, Roz Denny, Nicola Graimes, Becky Johnson,
Kim Morphew, Joy Skipper, Penny Stephens and Wendy Veale as well
as Weight Watchers Leaders and Members.

Photography by: Iain Bagwell, Steve Baxter, Steve Lee, Juliet Piddington
and William Shaw.
Project editor: Nicki Lampon.
Design and typesetting: Martin Lampon.

Colour reproduction by Dot Gradations Ltd, UK.
Printed and bound in China.

A CIP catalogue for this book is available from the British Library

ISBN 978-1-47111-090-0

1 2 3 4 5 6 7 8 9 10

Pictured on the title page: Thatched beef pie p74.
Pictured on the Introduction: Quick lamb stew p58, Steak and shallots in red wine
p48, Key lime pie p156.

WeightWatchers®

Fabulous recipes for evening meals

Satisfying Suppers

SIMON &
SCHUSTER
ILLUSTRATED

London · New York · Sydney · Toronto · New Delhi

A CBS COMPANY

Weight Watchers **ProPoints** Weight Loss System is a simple way to lose weight. As part of the Weight Watchers **ProPoints** plan you'll enjoy eating delicious, healthy, filling foods that help to keep you feeling satisfied for longer and in control of your portions.

ⓥ This symbol denotes a vegetarian recipe and assumes that, where relevant, free range eggs, vegetarian cheese, vegetarian virtually fat free fromage frais, vegetarian low fat crème fraîche and vegetarian low fat yogurts are used. Virtually fat free fromage frais, low fat crème fraîche and low fat yogurts may contain traces of gelatine so they are not always vegetarian. Please check the labels.

❄ This symbol denotes a dish that can be frozen. Unless otherwise stated, you can freeze the finished dish for up to 3 months. Defrost thoroughly and reheat until the dish is piping hot throughout.

Recipe notes

Egg size: Medium sized, unless otherwise stated.

Raw eggs: Only the freshest eggs should be used. Pregnant women, the elderly and children should avoid recipes with eggs that are not fully cooked or raw.

All fruits and vegetables: Medium sized, unless otherwise stated.

Stock: Stock cubes are used in recipes, unless otherwise stated. These should be prepared according to packet instructions.

Recipe timings: These are approximate and meant to be guidelines. Please note that the preparation time includes all the steps up to and following the main cooking time(s).

Microwaves: Timings and temperatures are for a standard 800 W microwave. If necessary, adjust your own microwave.

Low fat spread: Where a recipe states to use a low fat spread, a light spread with a fat content of no less than 38% should be used.

Low fat soft cheese: Where low fat soft cheese is specified in a recipe, this refers to soft cheese with a fat content of less than 5%.

Contents

Introduction

There is often so little time to cook a healthy meal in the evening, and it's far too easy to turn to take-aways or fast food for an easy, tasty fix. *Satisfying Suppers* is here to help, packed full of delicious, easy recipes from the best of Weight Watchers cookbooks. Some are quick to make and perfect for midweek meals, some take a little longer and are ideal for a weekend or when you have a little more time.

For a quick meal for the family try Salmon and Dill Fish Pie, Quick Lamb Stew or Pasta Pomodoro. Herby Chicken Calzone or Oriental-style Fish Parcels make a perfect meal for two, or feed a larger group with Chicken and Lentils with Wine and Herbs or Autumn Quiche. There are delicious desserts here too – perfect for finishing off a satisfying supper.

About Weight Watchers
For more than 40 years Weight Watchers has been helping people around the world to lose weight using a long term sustainable approach. Weight Watchers successful weight loss system is based on four tried and trusted principles:

- Eating healthily
- Being more active
- Adjusting behaviour to help weight loss
- Getting support in weekly meetings

Our unique *ProPoints* system empowers you to manage your food plan and make wise recipe choices for a healthier, happier you.

To find out more about Weight Watchers and the *ProPoints* values
for these recipes contact Customer Service on 0845 345 1500.

Storing and freezing

Making meals ahead of time and storing and freezing them is one of the keys to producing healthy tasty meals during a busy week. Many dishes store well in the fridge, but make sure you use them up within a day or two. Some can also be frozen. Try making double the quantity when you cook a recipe and storing the extra portions in the freezer. This way you'll always have a fantastic selection of meals that you can pull out and reheat at the end of a busy day. However, it is important to make sure you know how to freeze safely.

- Wrap any food to be frozen in rigid containers or strong freezer bags. This is important to stop foods contaminating each other or getting freezer burn.
- Label the containers or bags with the contents and date – your freezer should have a star marking that tells you how long you can keep different types of frozen food.
- Never freeze warm food – always let it cool completely first.
- Never freeze food that has already been frozen and defrosted.
- Freeze food in portions, then you can take out as little or as much as you need each time.
- Defrost what you need in the fridge, making sure you put anything that might have juices, such as meat, on a covered plate or in a container.
- Fresh food, such as raw meat and fish, should be wrapped and frozen as soon as possible.
- Most fruit and vegetables can be frozen by open freezing. Lay them out on a tray, freeze until solid and then pack them into bags.
- Some vegetables, such as peas, broccoli and broad beans, can be blanched first by cooking for 2 minutes in boiling water. Drain, refresh under cold water and then freeze once cold.

- Fresh herbs are great frozen – either seal leaves in bags or, for soft herbs such as basil and parsley, chop finely and add to ice cube trays with water. These are great for dropping into casseroles or soups straight from the freezer.

Some things cannot be frozen. Whole eggs do not freeze well, but yolks and whites can be frozen separately. Vegetables with a high water content, such as salad leaves, celery and cucumber, will not freeze. Fried foods will be soggy if frozen, and sauces such as mayonnaise will separate when thawed and should not be frozen.

Shopping hints and tips

Always buy the best ingredients you can afford. If you are going to cook healthy meals, it is worth investing in some quality ingredients that will really add flavour to your dishes. When buying meat, choose lean cuts of meat or lean mince, and if you are buying precooked sliced meat, buy it fresh from the deli counter.

When you're going around the supermarket it's tempting to pick up foods you like and put them in your trolley without thinking about how you will use them. So, a good plan is to decide what dishes you want to cook before you go shopping, check your store cupboard and make a list of what you need. You'll save time by not drifting aimlessly around the supermarket picking up what you fancy.

We've added a checklist here for some of the store cupboard ingredients used in this book. Just add fresh ingredients in your regular shop and you'll be ready to cook the wonderful recipes in *Satisfying Suppers*.

Store cupboard checklist

- [ ] almonds, flaked
- [ ] apricots, dried
- [ ] artificial sweetener
- [ ] bay leaves
- [ ] beans, canned
- [ ] black bean sauce
- [ ] capers, in a jar
- [ ] cardamom pods
- [ ] chestnut purée
- [ ] chick peas, canned
- [ ] chilli flakes
- [ ] chocolate, plain
- [ ] cinnamon, ground
- [ ] cocoa powder
- [ ] coconut milk, reduced fat
- [ ] cooking spray, calorie controlled
- [ ] coriander, ground
- [ ] cornflour
- [ ] couscous, dried
- [ ] crab meat, canned
- [ ] cumin (seeds and ground)
- [ ] curry pastes
- [ ] digestive biscuits, reduced fat
- [ ] fennel seeds
- [ ] flour, plain white
- [ ] garam masala
- [ ] golden syrup
- [ ] herbs, dried
- [ ] lentils, Puy
- [ ] mango chutney
- [ ] maple syrup
- [ ] mayonnaise, reduced fat
- [ ] mint sauce
- [ ] mustard (Dijon and wholegrain)
- [ ] mustard seeds
- [ ] noodles, dried
- [ ] oil (olive and vegetable)
- [ ] olives, stoned black in a jar
- [ ] paprika
- [ ] passata
- [ ] pasta, dried
- [ ] pear halves, canned in natural juice
- [ ] peppercorns
- [ ] pineapple, canned in natural juice
- [ ] pizza base mix
- [ ] rice, dried
- [ ] saffron strands
- [ ] salt
- [ ] sardines, canned
- [ ] soy sauce
- [ ] sponge fingers
- [ ] stock cubes
- [ ] stuffing mix
- [ ] sugar
- [ ] sweetcorn, canned
- [ ] Tabasco sauce
- [ ] tomato purée
- [ ] tomatoes, canned
- [ ] tuna, canned in brine
- [ ] turmeric
- [ ] vanilla essence
- [ ] vinegars
- [ ] Worcestershire sauce

Perfect poultry

Chicken roulades

Serves 2

245 calories per serving

Takes 15 minutes to prepare,
25 minutes to cook

❄

2 x 175 g (6 oz) skinless
boneless chicken breasts
75 g (2¾ oz) low fat soft
cheese
1 tablespoon finely chopped
fresh chives
½ teaspoon Dijon mustard
1 teaspoon sun-dried tomato
purée
calorie controlled cooking
spray

*Serve these lovely roulades with steamed vegetables, such
as mange tout and carrots.*

1 Preheat the oven to Gas Mark 4/180°C/fan oven 160°C. Line
a baking tray with non stick baking parchment.

2 Place each chicken breast between two pieces of
greaseproof paper and, using the flat end of a rolling pin,
hammer them out gently to about 1 cm (½ inch) thick. Peel
away the greaseproof paper and lay the breasts flat on a clean
work surface.

3 Beat together the soft cheese, chives, mustard and tomato
purée and spread equal amounts of this mixture over each
chicken breast. Loosely roll up the breasts from the narrow
end, enclosing the filling, and secure with one or two cocktail
sticks each.

4 Place the chicken rolls on the baking tray and spray with the
cooking spray. Cook for 25 minutes.

5 To serve, carefully remove the cocktail sticks. Slice each
breast into rings and arrange on warmed serving plates.

Tip... Hammer out the chicken breasts as evenly as
possible without splitting the flesh.

Turkey with tomato and chick pea sauce

Serves 4

210 calories per serving

Takes 10 minutes to prepare,
  25 minutes to cook

400 g can chopped tomatoes

410 g can chick peas, drained
  and rinsed

30 g (1¼ oz) stoned black
  olives in brine, drained and
  chopped

2 garlic cloves, crushed

2 teaspoons dried mixed herbs

150 ml (5 fl oz) chicken stock

4 x 110 g (4 oz) skinless
  boneless turkey breast
  steaks

*A delicious one pot bake with turkey steaks cooked on top
of an olive and garlic tomato sauce. Serve with a 150 g
(5½ oz) potato per person, baked in its skin, and steamed
broccoli.*

1 Preheat the oven to Gas Mark 5/190°C/fan oven 170°C.

2 Mix together the tomatoes, chick peas, olives, garlic, herbs
and stock. Pour into a shallow ovenproof dish or roasting tin.

3 Place the turkey steaks on top and bake for 25 minutes until
the steaks are beginning to brown. Serve.

Variation... Try this recipe with 4 x 125 g (4½ oz) skinless
boneless chicken breasts.

Tangy chicken with crushed potatoes

Serves 4
271 calories per serving
Takes 25 minutes
❄

600 g (1 lb 5 oz) baby new potatoes, scrubbed

4 x 125 g (4½ oz) skinless boneless chicken breasts, slashed

1 tablespoon Dijon mustard

1 tablespoon Worcestershire sauce

calorie controlled cooking spray

finely grated zest and juice of ½ a lemon

2 tablespoons chopped fresh parsley

2 teaspoons extra virgin olive oil

freshly ground black pepper

Tender sugar snap peas are a good vegetable to serve with this recipe.

1 Bring a pan of water to the boil, add the potatoes and cook for 15–20 minutes until tender. Preheat the grill to medium and line the grill pan with foil.

2 Meanwhile, season the chicken breasts with black pepper. Mix the mustard and Worcestershire sauce together and brush on to both sides of the chicken. Spray with the cooking spray and grill for 15 minutes, turning once, or until cooked through.

3 When the potatoes are ready, drain and then return to the pan. Use a wooden spoon to lightly crush the potatoes and mix in the lemon zest and juice, parsley, olive oil and some black pepper. Serve with the grilled chicken.

Tip... Slashing the chicken breasts with a sharp knife means that the flavours of the basting sauce can infuse the chicken, without the need for marinating.

Chicken balti

Serves 4
260 calories per serving
Takes 20 minutes to prepare,
  20 minutes to cook

calorie controlled cooking
  spray
4 x 150 g (5½ oz) skinless
  boneless chicken breasts,
  cubed
6 small new potatoes,
  scrubbed and quartered
1 onion, chopped finely
4 garlic cloves, crushed
5 cm (2 inches) fresh root
  ginger, chopped finely
400 g can chopped tomatoes
300 ml (10 fl oz) chicken stock
2 tablespoons balti curry
  paste
a bunch of fresh coriander,
  chopped
salt and freshly ground black
  pepper
4 lemon wedges, to serve

A mild, rich curry made with shop-bought balti paste to speed up the preparation. The flavours and textures are far fresher and more interesting than the usual take-away. Serve with 60 g (2 oz) dried basmati rice per person, cooked according to the packet instructions, and 1 tablespoon low fat natural yogurt per person.

1 Heat a large non stick frying pan and spray with the cooking spray. Stir-fry the chicken for 4 minutes until golden round the edges and white all over. Add the potatoes, onion, garlic and ginger and fry for a further 4 minutes until turning golden.

2 Add the tomatoes, stock and curry paste and bring to the boil. Simmer gently for 20 minutes until the chicken is tender and cooked through and the sauce thickened.

3 Stir in the coriander, adjust the seasoning if necessary and serve with the lemon wedges.

Saltimbocca

Serves 2
191 calories per serving
Takes 30 minutes

2 x 125 g (4½ oz) skinless turkey fillets
6 fresh sage leaves, plus extra to garnish
4 x 10 g (¼ oz) slices prosciutto
6 shallots, halved if large
300 ml (10 fl oz) hot chicken stock
salt and freshly ground black pepper

Traditionally made with veal, this version uses turkey fillets, which are flattened and rolled up with sage before being pan-fried and braised in stock. Serve with 60 g (2 oz) dried brown rice per person, cooked according to the packet instructions. Stir in 75 g (2¾ oz) spinach so that it just wilts.

1 Cover a chopping board with cling film and place the turkey fillets on top. Cover with another sheet of cling film and hammer gently with the flat end of a rolling pin until about 5 cm (2 inches) thick. Discard the cling film and season each fillet. Place 3 sage leaves and 2 slices of prosciutto on each fillet and roll up. If needs be, secure with a wooden cocktail stick.

2 Heat a lidded non stick frying pan until hot. Add the turkey roll ups, placing them seam side down, and brown slightly to lock in the flavour. Once sealed, add the shallots and turn the rolls so that they brown all over. Add the stock and bring to the boil. Cover and reduce to a simmer for 10 minutes until cooked through.

3 Remove the turkey to a plate, covering it with foil to keep it warm. Increase the heat and boil the sauce for 2–3 minutes until slightly reduced and thickened. Serve the turkey with the sauce, garnished with the extra sage leaves.

Sweet potato and turkey curry

Serves 4

263 calories per serving

Takes 20 minutes + marinating

450 g (1 lb) skinless boneless turkey breast, cut into bite size pieces

4 sweet potatoes, peeled and cubed

200 ml (7 fl oz) chicken stock

100 g (3½ oz) frozen spinach, defrosted

salt and freshly ground black pepper

a small bunch of fresh coriander, chopped, to garnish

For the marinade

2 teaspoons Thai red or green curry paste

2 tablespoons soy sauce

1 teaspoon caster sugar

100 ml (3½ fl oz) reduced fat coconut milk

grated zest and juice of a lime

2 red chillies, de-seeded and chopped finely

This curry will warm and cheer you up on a cold winter's evening. Serve with 1 chapati made without fat and 1 tablespoon low fat natural yogurt per person.

1 In a large bowl, mix together all the marinade ingredients except the lime juice, add the turkey and stir around until coated. Set aside to marinate for at least 30 minutes.

2 Bring a pan of water to the boil, add the sweet potatoes and cook until just tender.

3 Remove the turkey from the marinade and stir-fry in a wok or large non stick frying pan until browned. Add the cooked sweet potatoes, stock, leftover marinade and spinach. Cook for 10 minutes, but do not allow to boil. Stir in the lime juice, season and scatter with the coriander.

Paella pasta

Serves 4
412 calories per serving
Takes 27 minutes
❄

4 x 5 g thin slices chorizo, cut into strips

1 onion, chopped finely

2 garlic cloves, crushed

½ red pepper, de-seeded and sliced

500 g (1 lb 2 oz) skinless boneless chicken breasts, cubed

2 teaspoons paprika

a generous pinch of saffron strands

250 g (9 oz) dried rigatoni pasta

600 ml (20 fl oz) hot vegetable stock

230 g can chopped tomatoes

125 g (4½ oz) frozen peas

salt and freshly ground black pepper

lemon wedges, to serve

Inspired by the classic Spanish dish, this everyday version will soon become a family favourite.

1 Heat a deep, wide, lidded, non stick saucepan and add the chorizo, onion, garlic, red pepper and chicken. Cook for 5 minutes until starting to soften and brown, stirring occasionally. Stir in the paprika and saffron and cook for 30 seconds.

2 Stir in the pasta, stock and chopped tomatoes. Bring to the boil, cover and simmer for 9 minutes. Stir in the peas and cook for 2–3 minutes until the pasta is al dente and the stock has been absorbed. Check the seasoning and serve immediately with the lemon wedges.

Chicken and lentils with wine and herbs

Serves 8

418 calories per serving

Takes 20 minutes to prepare,
25 minutes to cook

8 fresh thyme sprigs

8 x 150 g (5½ oz) skinless
boneless chicken breasts

8 rashers lean back bacon

calorie controlled cooking
spray

2 red onions, sliced

4 garlic cloves, crushed

4 celery sticks, chopped

4 carrots, peeled and diced

300 g (10½ oz) dried Puy
lentils

1.2 litres (2 pints) chicken
stock

300 ml (10 fl oz) white wine

2 fresh rosemary sprigs

800 g (1 lb 11 oz) potatoes,
peeled and chopped

4 tablespoons chopped fresh
parsley, to garnish

Puy lentils are small and dark green and have a delicious flavour, particularly when cooked with wine and herbs.

1 Preheat the oven to Gas Mark 6/200°C/fan oven 180°C. Place a sprig of thyme on each chicken breast, wrap a bacon rasher around each one and place them in a non stick roasting tin. Spray with the cooking spray and bake for 20 minutes until golden and cooked through. (Insert a skewer and the juices should run clear. If not, return to the oven for another 5 minutes.)

2 Meanwhile, spray a lidded non stick saucepan with the cooking spray and heat until hot. Add the onions, garlic, celery and carrots with 2 tablespoons of water and cook for 3–4 minutes, stirring, until just softened.

3 Add the lentils, stock, wine and rosemary. Bring to the boil, cover and simmer for 20 minutes or until the lentils are tender. Add a little water if the mixture becomes too dry. Remove the rosemary.

4 Meanwhile, bring another saucepan of water to the boil, add the potatoes and cook for 15–20 minutes. Drain and mash.

5 Serve the chicken on a bed of lentils with a dollop of mash. Garnish with the parsley.

Coq au vin

Serves 4
210 calories per serving
Takes 25 minutes to prepare,
30 minutes to cook
❄

This classic French favourite tastes superb. It features chicken in a red wine sauce with mushrooms and shallots – making it a perfect meal anytime. Serve with 100 g (3½ oz) cooked new potatoes per person, accompanied by plenty of steamed vegetables, such as courgettes and broccoli.

calorie controlled cooking
  spray
8 shallots or small onions,
  halved
2 garlic cloves, crushed
4 x 140 g (5 oz) skinless
  boneless chicken breasts
125 ml (4 fl oz) red wine
300 ml (10 fl oz) chicken stock
175 g (6 oz) button
  mushrooms, halved
1 bay leaf
1 tablespoon cornflour
salt and freshly ground black
  pepper

1 Heat a large, lidded, non stick frying pan and spray with the cooking spray. Add the shallots or onions and garlic and sauté for about 5 minutes, until they begin to turn brown. Push them to one side of the pan.

2 Add the chicken breasts to the pan and seal them quickly on both sides. Pour in the wine and let it bubble up for a few seconds. Add the chicken stock, mushrooms and bay leaf. Cover and simmer gently for about 30 minutes, until the chicken is tender.

3 Blend the cornflour to a paste with 3 tablespoons of water and stir into the pan. Heat, stirring constantly, until the sauce is thickened and smooth. Check the seasoning, remove the bay leaf and serve on warmed plates.

Turkey and cranberry burgers

Serves 4
288 calories per serving
Takes 25 minutes
❄

450 g (1 lb) minced turkey
2 tablespoons cranberry sauce
50 g (1¾ oz) fresh wholemeal
   breadcrumbs
1 egg
4 spring onions, sliced thinly
salt and freshly ground black
   pepper

To serve
4 burger buns
¼ Iceberg lettuce, shredded
4 tomato slices

As we all know, turkey and cranberries are the perfect combination, so there is no reason why we should reserve them just for Christmas.

1 Preheat the grill to medium. Place the minced turkey in a large mixing bowl and add the cranberry sauce, breadcrumbs, egg, spring onions and seasoning. Using clean hands, combine the mixture together thoroughly.

2 Divide the mixture into four and shape into burgers. Grill the burgers for 15 minutes, turning halfway through the cooking time.

3 To serve, split the burger buns in half and place a cooked burger in each with a little shredded lettuce and a tomato slice.

Tip... Burgers are always a welcome speedy snack, but home-made ones are so much more tasty than the shop-bought variety. Make a double batch and freeze them individually, then you'll always have some fast food available.

Herby chicken calzone

Serves 2

307 calories per serving

Takes 35 minutes to prepare,
15 minutes to cook

❄

calorie controlled cooking
  spray

½ x 144 g packet pizza base
  mix

2 teaspoons dried mixed herbs

250 g (9 oz) skinless boneless
  chicken breast, cut into
  strips

1 courgette, grated

4 cherry tomatoes, halved

10 fresh basil leaves

2 tablespoons sun-dried
  tomato purée

1 egg white, beaten lightly, to
  glaze

A calzone is a folded pizza, similar to a Cornish pasty in appearance.

1 Preheat the oven to Gas Mark 7/220°C/fan oven 200°C. Spray a non stick baking tray with the cooking spray and set aside.

2 Make up the pizza dough according to the packet instructions, adding the dried herbs before the water. Knead for 5 minutes, return the dough to the mixing bowl, cover with a clean cloth and leave to prove while you prepare the filling.

3 Spray a non stick frying pan with the cooking spray, heat until sizzling and then add the chicken. Cook over a medium heat, stirring occasionally, for 5 minutes until the chicken is golden and cooked through. Add the courgette and cook for 1 minute to allow some of the water to evaporate. Remove from the heat. Mix in the tomatoes and basil.

4 Divide the dough in two and knead each piece lightly. Shape into two rounds approximately 18 cm (7 inches) in diameter and place on the baking tray. Spread the tomato purée over the bases and place the filling on one side of each circle. Brush the edges with a little water, fold over and pinch the edges together to seal. Leave in a warm place to prove for 5 minutes.

5 Brush with the egg white and bake for 15 minutes until golden. Serve either warm or cold.

Turkey tomato pasta

Serves 4

270 calories per serving

Takes 10 minutes to prepare,
20 minutes to cook

2 teaspoons olive oil

a bunch of spring onions,
sliced finely

1 garlic clove, crushed

1 green pepper, de-seeded and
chopped

4 plum or ordinary tomatoes,
chopped

50 g (1¾ oz) sun-dried
tomatoes in oil, rinsed and
sliced

200 ml (7 fl oz) tomato juice or
passata

1 tablespoon dried oregano or
Italian herbs

175 g (6 oz) dried pasta
shapes

150 g (5½ oz) turkey rashers

salt and freshly ground black
pepper

a handful of fresh oregano
or basil leaves, to garnish
(optional)

*Turkey rashers are very low in fat and they're tasty too.
They make an excellent addition to this easy pasta dish,
which the whole family, including children, will love.*

1 Heat the oil in a large non stick saucepan and sauté the
spring onions and garlic until softened, about 2 minutes. Add
the pepper and cook, stirring, for another 2 minutes.

2 Add the fresh and sun-dried tomatoes, tomato juice or
passata and dried herbs. Heat until bubbling and then turn the
heat to low and simmer for 10 minutes. Preheat the grill to
high.

3 Meanwhile, bring a pan of water to the boil, add the pasta
and cook for 8–10 minutes, until just tender.

4 At the same time, grill the turkey rashers for 1½ minutes on
each side and then snip into small pieces.

5 Drain the pasta well and then add the sauce and most of the
turkey rashers. Season to taste. Divide between four warmed
plates and garnish with the oregano or basil leaves, if using,
and the reserved turkey rashers. Sprinkle with black pepper
and serve at once.

Variation... If you like, you can replace the fresh tomatoes
and tomato juice or passata with a 400 g can of chopped
tomatoes.

Chicken curry with almonds

Serves 4
368 calories per serving
Takes 20 minutes to prepare, 25 minutes to cook

Serve this creamy curry with 60 g (2 oz) dried brown rice per person, cooked according to the packet instructions.

1 teaspoon coriander seeds
calorie controlled cooking spray
4 x 150 g (5½ oz) skinless boneless chicken breasts, diced
2 onions, chopped finely
3 garlic cloves, chopped finely
2.5 cm (1 inch) fresh root ginger, chopped finely
½ teaspoon cumin seeds
½ teaspoon fennel seeds
½ teaspoon mustard seeds

½ teaspoon turmeric
½ teaspoon dried chilli flakes
1 cardamom pod
1 large potato (approximately 250 g/9 oz), peeled and diced
300 ml (10 fl oz) chicken stock
100 g (3½ oz) baby spinach, washed
300 g (10½ oz) low fat natural yogurt
a bunch of fresh coriander, chopped
salt and freshly ground black pepper
50 g (1¾ oz) flaked almonds, toasted, to serve

1 Crush the coriander seeds in a pestle and mortar or spice grinder. Spray a large, lidded, non stick pan with the cooking spray and place on a high heat. Add the chicken pieces, season and brown on all sides. Remove to a plate.

2 Spray the pan again and stir-fry the onions, garlic, ginger and spices, including the crushed coriander seeds, until the onion is softened, adding a splash of water if necessary to prevent them from sticking. Add the potato, chicken and stock, stir and scrape up any bits stuck on the bottom of the pan. Cover, simmer for 20 minutes and then remove from the heat.

3 Stir in the spinach, leave to wilt for 5 minutes and then stir in the yogurt and coriander. Season to taste and scatter with the toasted almonds to serve.

Chicken and ham pancake pie

Serves 4

319 calories per serving

Takes 20 minutes to prepare,
15–20 minutes to cook

❄ (see Tip)

**128 g packet pancake batter
mix**

1 egg

**calorie controlled cooking
spray**

1 leek, sliced

**2 x 150 g (5½ oz) skinless
boneless chicken breasts,
cut into 2 cm (¾ inch) pieces**

**500 g jar creamy mushroom
sauce**

**125 g (4½ oz) thick sliced
cooked ham, chopped**

**1 tablespoon chopped fresh
chives**

freshly ground black pepper

*Here is a clever, quick way to make a substantial 'pie' with
a new twist: tasty pancake-lined ramekins, bubbling with a
creamy traditional filling. Be sure to use the whole packet
of pancake batter mix for thick, satisfying pancakes. Serve
with steamed carrots and broccoli.*

1 Preheat the oven to Gas Mark 5/180°C/fan oven 160°C.
Make the pancake batter according to the packet instructions,
adding the egg.

2 Spray a 20 cm (8 inch) non stick omelette pan with the
cooking spray, add a quarter of the batter and cook until
golden, turning over halfway through. Repeat to make four
pancakes.

3 Meanwhile, dry-fry the leek and chicken in a non stick
frying pan for 5 minutes, or until the chicken has coloured.
Stir in the mushroom sauce and ham and heat through for
2 minutes. Season with black pepper and stir in the chives.

4 Line four 10 cm (4 inch) bowls or ramekin dishes with
a pancake each. Divide the chicken mixture between the
ramekins and fold in the overhanging pancakes to partly
conceal the filling.

5 Cook for 15–20 minutes until the filling is bubbling and the
edges are crispy. Serve immediately.

**Tip... To freeze, wrap pancakes individually between layers
of greaseproof paper and freeze them for up to 6 months.
Simply remove one or two at a time as required. If freezing
the pancakes filled (after step 4), cover and freeze for up to
6 weeks. Defrost thoroughly before cooking.**

Pot roast chicken

Serves 4

327 calories per serving

Takes 30 minutes to prepare,
20–25 minutes to cook

**calorie controlled cooking
spray**

**4 x 135 g (5 oz) chicken
quarters, with skin on**

6–8 small shallots

100 ml (3½ fl oz) white wine

**1 litre (1¾ pints) hot chicken
or vegetable stock**

**2 tablespoons sun-dried
tomato purée**

**1 teaspoon dried
Mediterranean herbs,
e.g. oregano, marjoram
and/or basil**

**400 g (14 oz) new potatoes,
scrubbed and quartered or
halved if large**

**2 large carrots, peeled and cut
into 1 cm (½ inch) diagonal
slices**

2 celery sticks, chopped

**salt and freshly ground black
pepper**

**a large bunch of fresh
tarragon or basil, chopped,
to serve**

*Ideal for a winter's evening and best served with lots
of green vegetables such as steamed broccoli, beans or
spinach.*

1 Heat a large, lidded, ovenproof casserole dish, spray with
the cooking spray and fry the chicken quarters for 10 minutes
on each side, until golden all over. Season.

2 Preheat the oven to Gas Mark 6/200°C/fan oven 180°C.
Add the shallots to the casserole dish and fry for a further
10 minutes, until golden. Add the white wine and boil rapidly,
scraping up any browned juices from the base of the pan.

3 Remove the dish from the hob and add all the other
ingredients except the fresh tarragon or basil. Cover and roast
for 20–25 minutes until the juices run clear when the joints are
stuck with a skewer in the thickest part of the thigh.

4 Check the seasoning, remove the skin from the chicken
quarters and serve the chicken sprinkled with the chopped
tarragon or basil.

Mediterranean chicken

Serves 4

370 calories per serving

Takes 25 minutes to prepare,
25 minutes to cook

- **1 tablespoon olive or vegetable oil**
- **1 red onion, sliced**
- **2 celery sticks, sliced**
- **4 x 150 g (5½ oz) skinless boneless chicken breasts**
- **125 ml (4 fl oz) red wine**
- **150 ml (5 fl oz) chicken stock**
- **12 small stoned black olives in brine, drained and halved (optional)**
- **25 g (1 oz) raisins or sultanas**
- **2 fresh rosemary sprigs, plus extra to garnish (optional)**
- **2 fresh thyme sprigs, plus extra to garnish (optional)**
- **125 g (4½ oz) dried long grain rice**
- **salt and freshly ground black pepper**

Lean chicken breasts take on an Italian flavour in this easy to cook dish.

1 Heat the oil in a large, lidded, non stick frying pan and sauté the onion and celery for 2 minutes. Add the chicken breasts and cook for 3–4 minutes more, turning once, to brown.

2 Add the wine, stock, olives, if using, raisins or sultanas, rosemary and thyme. Season. Bring to the boil, reduce the heat, cover and simmer for about 25 minutes, until the chicken is tender.

3 Meanwhile, bring a pan of water to the boil, add the rice and cook according to the packet instructions.

4 Drain the rice and serve with the chicken, garnished with the extra rosemary and thyme sprigs, if using.

Variation... Use white wine instead of red if you prefer.

Maple and mustard chicken traybake

Serves 4

387 calories per serving

Takes 15 minutes to prepare, 40 minutes to cook.

800 g (1 lb 11 oz) small new potatoes, scrubbed and halved

2 red onions, chopped roughly

2 courgettes, chopped roughly

1 tablespoon olive oil

4 x 125 g (4½ oz) skinless, boneless chicken breasts

2 tablespoons maple syrup

1 heaped tablespoon wholegrain mustard

juice of a lemon

250 g (9 oz) cherry tomatoes

salt and freshly ground black pepper

Great for a midweek roast, this also cuts down on washing up as it's all cooked together in one tray.

1 Preheat the oven to Gas Mark 6/200°C/fan oven 180°C.

2 Bring a pan of water to the boil, add the potatoes and cook for 10 minutes. Drain and mix with the onions, courgettes, olive oil and seasoning in a large non stick roasting tin. Place in the oven to cook for 15 minutes.

3 Season the chicken breasts. Stir the vegetables around and add the chicken to the roasting tin. Roast for a further 10 minutes.

4 Mix the maple syrup with the mustard and lemon juice. Stir the vegetables around again, adding the tomatoes, and drizzle the maple mustard glaze all over the chicken and vegetables. Roast for a final 15 minutes.

Marvellous meat

Sausage and lentil casserole

Serves 4

325 calories per serving

Takes 15 minutes to prepare,
  30 minutes to cook

❄

450 g (1 lb) reduced fat pork
  sausages
1 large onion, chopped
1 garlic clove, crushed
1 large carrot, peeled and
  grated coarsely
175 g (6 oz) dried Puy lentils
a few fresh thyme sprigs
400 g can chopped tomatoes
600 ml (20 fl oz) hot beef
  stock
4 tablespoons half fat crème
  fraîche
salt and freshly ground black
  pepper

*How about preparing this recipe for Guy Fawkes night?
It can be made well in advance, leaving you time to
concentrate on other noisier bangers on the night. Serve
with a generous spoonful of mashed swede.*

1 Prick the sausages all over and dry-fry in a non stick
saucepan until lightly coloured. Add the onion to the pan and
continue to stir-fry until the onion is softened and golden. Add
the garlic and carrot and cook for a further minute.

2 Stir in the lentils, thyme sprigs, tomatoes and stock. Bring
to the boil, reduce the heat to a gentle simmer and cook,
uncovered, for 30 minutes. Stir occasionally, adding a drop of
water if the mixture becomes too dry. Season to taste.

3 When the casserole is ready to serve, stir in the crème
fraîche.

Tip... You can find Puy lentils in good supermarkets. They
require no soaking and taste great. Otherwise, green lentils
or continental lentils are a good substitute.

Ⓥ **Variation...** For a vegetarian option, use 2 x 250 g
packets of Quorn Sausages and vegetable stock.

Steak and shallots in red wine

Serves 2

293 calories per serving

Takes 5 minutes to prepare,
20 minutes to cook

8 shallots, quartered

calorie controlled cooking
spray

2 x 150 g (5½ oz) sirloin
steaks, trimmed of visible fat

4 tablespoons balsamic
vinegar

150 ml (5 fl oz) red wine

150 ml (5 fl oz) beef or
vegetable stock

salt and freshly ground black
pepper

*Serve this special dinner for two with mashed potato
(200 g/7 oz boiled potatoes mashed with 2 tablespoons of
skimmed milk per person), and a green vegetable such as
green beans.*

1 Bring a pan of water to the boil, add the shallots and simmer
for 2–3 minutes. Drain and set aside.

2 Spray a non stick frying pan with the cooking spray, season
the steaks and fry for 3–4 minutes on each side, or until
cooked to your liking.

3 Remove the steaks to a plate and keep warm. Add the
shallots to the pan and stir-fry until browned. Add the
balsamic vinegar and allow to bubble while you scrape up all
the stuck on bits.

4 Add the wine and boil until the sauce is sticky. Add the
stock and simmer for a few minutes until thickened.

5 Spoon the shallots and sauce over the steaks and serve
immediately.

Ⓥ **Variation...** For a vegetarian version, see the recipe on
page 139.

Creamy lamb, spinach and chick pea stir-fry

Serves 4
250 calories per serving
Takes 30 minutes

300 g (10½ oz) lean lamb steak, trimmed of visible fat and sliced into strips

6 spring onions, sliced

175 g (6 oz) baby spinach, kale or purple sprouting broccoli

1 teaspoon cornflour

175 g (6 oz) canned chick peas, drained and rinsed

400 g can chopped tomatoes

1 tablespoon chopped fresh chives or parsley

150 g (5½ oz) low fat natural yogurt

salt and freshly ground black pepper

This is good eaten with 60 g (2 oz) dried basmati rice per person, cooked according to the packet instructions, or a plain Weight Watchers mini naan bread per person. Serve accompanied with fresh green vegetables – green beans or courgettes go well.

1 Dry-fry the lamb in a large non stick frying pan for 4–5 minutes. Add the spring onions and spinach, kale or broccoli and stir-fry for a further 2 minutes.

2 Blend the cornflour to a paste with a little cold water and stir in with the chick peas, tomatoes and chives or parsley. Season and cook for a further 10 minutes.

3 Stir in the yogurt, just sufficiently to warm it through, and then serve.

Ginger and mustard pork

Serves 2
213 calories per serving
Takes 10 minutes to prepare,
  15 minutes to cook

250 g (9 oz) pork escalopes,
  trimmed of visible fat and
  cut into 6–8 pieces
calorie controlled cooking
  spray
1 red onion, sliced into rings
3 slices fresh root ginger, each
  about the size of a pound
  coin
1 garlic clove, crushed
150 ml (5 fl oz) chicken stock
1 teaspoon Tabasco sauce
2 teaspoons wholegrain
  mustard
1 tablespoon maple syrup
salt and freshly ground black
  pepper

Quick and easy, this is a perfect dish for a midweek meal.

1 Heat a large non stick frying pan to a high temperature and quickly brown the pork pieces on both sides. (You won't need any oil at this stage.) Remove the pork and keep warm on a covered plate.

2 Reduce the heat of the pan, spray it with the cooking spray and add the onion, ginger and garlic. Cook for 3–5 minutes until soft and starting to brown.

3 Add the stock, Tabasco sauce and mustard, bring to a gentle simmer and then return the pork to the pan. Cook for 5–10 minutes until the pork is cooked through.

4 Remove the slices of ginger and stir in the maple syrup. Season to taste and serve on warmed plates.

Tip... For a different mashed potato, peel 350 g (12 oz) potatoes and 200 g (7 oz) celeriac and chop into chunks. Boil together for 15 minutes and then add a peeled, cored and sliced dessert apple and boil for another 5 minutes or until everything is just soft enough to mash. Drain and mash with a little skimmed milk.

Beef, mushroom and potato moussaka

Serves 4

485 calories per serving

Takes 25 minutes to prepare,
35 minutes to cook

600 g (1 lb 5 oz) potatoes,
  peeled

calorie controlled cooking
  spray

500 g (1 lb 2 oz) extra lean
  minced beef

2 garlic cloves, crushed

200 g (7 oz) mushrooms,
  chopped

400 g can chopped tomatoes

1 tablespoon tomato purée

2 eggs, beaten

150 g (5½ oz) 0% fat Greek
  yogurt

100 g (3½ oz) half fat Cheddar
  cheese, grated

salt and freshly ground black
  pepper

*It's worth parboiling the potatoes in this recipe since it
drastically reduces the cooking time.*

1 Preheat the oven to Gas Mark 4/180°C/fan oven 160°C.

2 Bring a pan of water to the boil, add the potatoes and cook
for 5 minutes. Drain, allow to cool and then slice thinly.

3 Heat a non stick pan, spray with the cooking spray and
brown the minced beef, garlic and mushrooms. Add the
tomatoes and tomato purée and simmer for 5 minutes.
Season to taste.

4 Put half of this mixture in an ovenproof dish and cover with
half of the potatoes. Repeat with the remaining meat and
potatoes.

5 Beat the eggs, yogurt and cheese together and use this to
top the moussaka. Bake, uncovered, for 35 minutes.

Variation... You can jazz this recipe up so that it is suitable
for a supper party by substituting wild mushrooms for the
mushrooms in the recipe.

Steak au poivre

Serves 2
345 calories per serving
Takes 15 minutes +
  marinating
❄

1 heaped teaspoon
  peppercorns
2 x 175 g (6 oz) rump or
  entrecote steaks, each
  2.5 cm (1 inch) thick and
  trimmed of visible fat
2 teaspoons olive oil
2 shallots, chopped
5 tablespoons beef or
  vegetable stock
30 ml (1 fl oz) brandy
2 tablespoons half fat crème
  fraîche

This classic recipe is still the all-time favourite way of eating steak for many people. It is delicious with a fresh, peppery watercress salad.

1 Crush the peppercorns in a pestle and mortar or spice mill and rub into both sides of the steaks, pressing them in with your hand. Cover with foil and leave as long as possible, for up to 3 hours.

2 Heat a non stick pan, add the olive oil and fry the steaks for 4–5 minutes for medium done. Remove from the pan and set aside, keeping warm, while you make the sauce.

3 Fry the shallots for 2 minutes in the oil and meat juices remaining in the pan and then add the stock and brandy and cook rapidly, scraping up the juices from the bottom of the pan and stirring in. Add the crème fraîche, bring to the boil, pour over the steaks and serve.

Variation... This recipe is also absolutely delicious made with fresh tuna steaks rather than beef.

Quick lamb stew

Serves 4
283 calories per serving
Takes 23 minutes
❄

4 x 150 g (5½ oz) lean lamb leg steaks, trimmed of visible fat

calorie controlled cooking spray

1 onion, chopped

1 garlic clove, sliced

2 tablespoons tomato purée

1 tablespoon dried herbes de Provence

400 g can chopped tomatoes

400 g can flageolet beans, drained and rinsed

grated zest of ½ a lemon

1 tablespoon finely chopped fresh flat leaf parsley

10 stoned black olives in brine, drained and sliced

salt and freshly ground black pepper

These tender lamb steaks served in a rich tomato ragu are delicious with lots of green vegetables.

1 Heat a deep, wide, lidded non stick saucepan and spray the lamb with the cooking spray. Cook the lamb for 5 minutes until browned all over. Remove and set aside.

2 Add the onion and garlic to the pan and cook for 3 minutes until starting to soften. Add the tomato purée and herbes de Provence and cook for 30 seconds. Stir in the chopped tomatoes and flageolet beans and return the lamb to the pan.

3 Cover and cook gently for 10 minutes, stirring occasionally. Check the seasoning and then stir in the lemon zest, parsley and olives. Serve immediately.

Tip... If you like your lamb well done, simmer for 5 minutes longer.

Tandoori lamb

Serves 2
242 calories per serving
Takes 50 minutes
❄ (lamb only)

2 teaspoons tandoori curry paste

2 tablespoons chopped fresh coriander

1 tablespoon smooth mango chutney

2 x 100 g (3½ oz) lean lamb leg steaks, trimmed of visible fat

200 g (7 oz) new potatoes, such as Charlotte or Jersey Royal, scrubbed and halved

75 g (2¾ oz) low fat natural yogurt

1 tablespoon mint sauce

75 g (2¾ oz) cucumber, de-seeded and diced

½ small red onion, sliced finely

Serve with a plain Weight Watchers mini naan bread per person and a mixed leaf salad.

1 To make the marinade, mix together the tandoori paste, coriander and mango chutney in a non metallic bowl. Add the lamb steaks and coat in the marinade. Set aside for 30 minutes.

2 Meanwhile, bring a lidded pan of water to the boil, add the potatoes and simmer, covered, for 20 minutes until tender. Drain and leave to cool.

3 Preheat the grill to medium. Put the lamb on a foil-lined grill pan and grill for 8–12 minutes, turning halfway until charred and cooked to your liking. Remove from the grill, cover loosely with foil and set aside.

4 Mix together the yogurt, mint sauce, cucumber and onion with the potatoes. Serve with the tandoori lamb.

Rich beef stew

Serves 4

340 calories per serving

Takes 35 minutes to prepare,
 1 hour to cook

❄

400 g (14 oz) extra lean beef,
 trimmed of visible fat and
 cubed

calorie controlled cooking
 spray

2 large onions, chopped

2 garlic cloves, peeled

100 g (3½ oz) ready-to-eat
 dried apricots, chopped

8 sun-dried tomatoes, sliced

400 g can chopped tomatoes

600 g (1 lb 5 oz) floury
 potatoes, peeled and cubed
 e.g. Maris Piper, King Edward

salt and freshly ground black
 pepper

a bunch of fresh parsley,
 chopped, to serve (optional)

*A dark, thick stew with a tang of fruit and tomato. You
could also serve this with a 225 g (8 oz) potato per person,
baked in its skin.*

1 Heat a non stick frying pan and dry-fry the beef over a high
heat until it is browned all over. Remove from the heat and
set aside.

2 Spray the pan with the cooking spray and reduce the heat
to medium. Fry the onions and garlic for 4 minutes until
softened. Return the meat to the pan, scatter over the apricots
and sun-dried tomatoes and season well.

3 Add the canned tomatoes and 600 ml (20 fl oz) of water and
bring to the boil. Reduce the heat and simmer for 1 hour until
thick and rich, stirring occasionally.

4 Meanwhile, bring a pan of water to the boil, add the potatoes
and cook until tender. Drain and serve with the stew, scattered
with the parsley, if using.

Variation... You could use dried prunes, raisins or dates
instead of the apricots.

Quick roast pork fillet

Serves 4
273 calories per serving
Takes 35 minutes

3 garlic cloves, crushed
3 tablespoons snipped fresh chives
3 tablespoons chopped fresh thyme
500 g (1 lb 2 oz) lean pork fillet, trimmed of visible fat
15 g (½ oz) low fat spread
3 leeks, sliced
150 ml (5 fl oz) chicken stock
200 g (7 oz) frozen peas
50 g (1¾ oz) low fat soft cheese
freshly ground black pepper

Serve with 200 g (7 oz) cooked potatoes (mashed with 2 tablespoons of skimmed milk) per person.

1 Preheat the oven to Gas Mark 6/200°C/fan oven 180°C.

2 Mix together two crushed garlic cloves with the chives and half the thyme. Roll the pork fillet in the garlic and herb mixture to coat. Place on a non stick roasting tray and roast in the oven for 25 minutes until cooked through but still juicy – the juices should run clear when the thickest part of the pork is pierced with a sharp knife or skewer.

3 After the pork has been cooking for 15 minutes, melt the low fat spread in a lidded non stick saucepan. Stir in the leeks, remaining garlic and 3 tablespoons of stock. Cover the pan and cook for 3 minutes. Pour in the rest of the stock, add the peas and cook, covered, for a further 5 minutes.

4 Mix the soft cheese and remaining thyme into the leeks and peas. Season with black pepper and serve with the pork, carved into thick slices.

Sausage and fennel pasta

Serves 4
338 calories per serving
Takes 25 minutes

6 **Weight Watchers Premium Pork Sausages**
200 g (7 oz) dried wholemeal penne pasta
calorie controlled cooking spray
1 onion, diced
1 fennel bulb, sliced thinly
198 g can sweetcorn, drained
finely grated zest of a small lemon

Fennel has a light aniseed flavour and is used in a lot of Italian recipes. It can also be used raw in salad and pasta dishes.

1 Preheat the grill to medium and cook the sausages for 10–15 minutes, turning regularly, until brown and cooked through.

2 At the same time, bring a large pan of water to the boil. Add the pasta and cook according to the packet instructions. Drain, reserving 4 tablespoons of the cooking liquid.

3 Meanwhile, spray a non stick frying pan with the cooking spray and heat until hot. Add the onion and fennel and stir-fry for 4 minutes until just tender.

4 Return the pasta to the pan with the reserved cooking liquid, onion and fennel mixture and sweetcorn. Chop the sausages into bite size pieces and add to the pan with the lemon zest. Heat through gently until piping hot.

❤ **Variation...** For a vegetarian version, use a 250 g packet of Quorn sausages, instead of the pork sausages.

Spanish meatballs

Serves 4
295 calories per serving
Takes 20 minutes to prepare,
   45 minutes to cook
❄

400 g (14 oz) minced lamb
1 onion, grated coarsely
3 garlic cloves, crushed
1 egg
30 g (1¼ oz) ground almonds
1 teaspoon paprika
1 tablespoon ground cumin
¼ teaspoon ground cinnamon
a small bunch of fresh parsley,
   chopped finely
salt and freshly ground black
   pepper

For the sauce
1 tablespoon fennel seeds
150 ml (5 fl oz) apple juice
400 g can chopped tomatoes
1 tablespoon tomato purée

*Spanish meatballs, or albondigas, are found everywhere in
Spain. Serve with 60 g (2 oz) dried basmati rice per person,
cooked according to the packet instructions.*

1 Put all the main ingredients into a bowl and mix thoroughly.
Using wet hands, take small handfuls of the mixture and roll
into 20 walnut size balls.

2 To make the sauce, dry-fry the fennel seeds for 2 minutes
in a wide, large, lidded, non stick pan. Add the apple juice
and boil for 2 minutes and then add the tomatoes and tomato
purée with 150 ml (5 fl oz) of water. Season and simmer
gently for 10 minutes.

3 Add the meatballs and make sure they are all covered by
the sauce. Cover and simmer for 20–30 minutes. Turn them
carefully once or twice during cooking and add more water if
needed.

Pineapple and pork burgers

Serves 4
377 calories per serving
Takes 22 minutes
❄ (burgers only before cooking)

500 g (1 lb 2 oz) lean minced pork
½ x 85 g packet dried sage and onion stuffing mix
2 x 50 g (1¾ oz) burger buns, halved
calorie controlled cooking spray
1 small apple, cored and cut into matchsticks
2 teaspoons reduced fat mayonnaise
50 g (1¾ oz) 0% fat Greek yogurt
227 g can pineapple slices in natural juice, drained
60 g (2 oz) half fat mature Cheddar cheese, grated
salt and freshly ground black pepper

Finish each burger with a small handful of shredded spinach, half a sliced tomato and some sliced red onion and serve each with 100 g (3½ oz) low fat, thick cut oven chips.

1 In a bowl, mix together the pork, stuffing mix and seasoning until combined. Using wet hands, shape the mixture into four burgers. Preheat the grill to medium high.

2 Put the burger buns on a foil-lined grill pan and cook under the grill for 1–2 minutes until toasted. Remove and set aside.

3 Put the burgers on the grill pan, spray with the cooking spray and cook for 12 minutes, turning halfway through the cooking time, until cooked.

4 Meanwhile, in a bowl, to make an 'appleslaw', mix together the apple, mayonnaise, yogurt and seasoning. Set aside.

5 Remove the burgers from the grill and top each with a pineapple slice and a quarter of the cheese. Return to the grill and cook for 1–2 minutes until the cheese is just melted. Serve each burger on a bun half and top with the appleslaw.

Beef with peppers and black bean sauce

Serves 2
298 calories per serving
Takes 15 minutes

2 teaspoons sunflower oil

250 g (9 oz) lean beef fillet, trimmed of visible fat and cut into strips

1 onion, sliced

1 green pepper, de-seeded and chopped roughly

1 garlic clove, sliced

1 cm (½ inch) fresh root ginger, cut into matchsticks

1 red chilli, de-seeded and sliced

120 g sachet black bean sauce

The salty, savoury flavour of black bean sauce works particularly well with beef, and fresh red chilli gives this an extra kick. Serve with 60 g (2 oz) dried noodles, cooked according to the packet instructions.

1 Heat the oil in a wok or large non stick frying pan until smoking hot. Add the beef strips and onion and stir-fry for 2 minutes.

2 Add all the remaining ingredients except the black bean sauce and stir-fry for 3 minutes.

3 Pour in the black bean sauce along with 2 tablespoons of water and heat through. Serve immediately.

Tip... Black bean sauce is available in sachets from most large supermarkets.

Spiced lamb steaks with couscous

Serves 2
288 calories per serving
Takes 12 minutes

grated zest and juice of
  ½ a lemon
1 red chilli, de-seeded and
  diced
1 teaspoon cumin seeds
2 x 150 g (5½ oz) lean lamb
  steaks, trimmed of visible fat
calorie controlled cooking
  spray
100 g (3½ oz) dried couscous
175 ml (6 fl oz) boiling water
2 tablespoons fresh coriander,
  chopped
salt and freshly ground black
  pepper

*Cumin is a classic Middle Eastern spice that goes
particularly well with lamb.*

1 On a plate, mix together the lemon zest, half the chilli, the
cumin seeds and some seasoning. Press the lamb steaks into
the mixture to coat the meat.

2 Lightly spray a non stick frying pan with the cooking spray
and fry the lamb steaks for 3–4 minutes on each side, until
done to your liking.

3 Meanwhile, mix the lemon juice and remaining chilli into
the couscous in a bowl. Season and add the boiling water. Stir
the mixture, cover the bowl and leave the couscous to stand for
5 minutes to soften.

4 Fluff up the couscous with a fork and mix in the coriander.
Slice the lamb steaks and serve on a bed of couscous.

Thatched beef pie

Serves 6

326 calories per serving

Takes 30 minutes to prepare,
25 minutes to cook

calorie controlled cooking
spray

500 g (1 lb 2 oz) extra lean
minced beef

1 onion, chopped finely

1 tablespoon plain white flour

300 ml (10 fl oz) hot beef
stock

a few shakes of
Worcestershire sauce

415 g can reduced sugar and
salt baked beans

freshly ground black pepper

For the thatch topping

900 g (2 lb) potatoes, washed
and all the same size
(medium)

3 carrots, peeled and grated
coarsely

40 g (1½ oz) half fat mature
Cheddar cheese, grated

*This makes a pleasant change from cottage pie but is still
very family friendly. It can easily be prepared earlier in the
day, ready to pop in the oven at tea time.*

1 Preheat the oven to Gas Mark 5/190°C/fan oven 170°C.

2 Heat a large, lidded, non stick saucepan until hot and spray
with the cooking spray. Add the minced beef and onion and
cook for 5 minutes over a high heat, stirring to break up. Add
the flour, followed by the stock and stir. Season with black
pepper and add a few shakes of Worcestershire sauce. Cover,
simmer gently for 15 minutes and then stir in the baked beans.

3 Meanwhile, bring a lidded saucepan of water to the boil, add
the potatoes and cook for 12 minutes.

4 Heat a non stick frying pan and spray with the cooking spray.
Add the carrots and stir-fry for 3–4 minutes until softened. Tip
into a mixing bowl.

5 Drain the potatoes, cover with cold water and cool for
2 minutes. Drain again and then scrape off the skins using a
table knife. Grate coarsely and add to the carrots, using two
forks to mix together.

6 Tip the mince into a large ovenproof baking dish. Spoon the
potato and carrot mixture on top and sprinkle with the cheese.
Bake for 25 minutes until the topping is golden and crisp.

Tip... Make sure you use medium potatoes and leave them
whole. Cutting large potatoes in half doesn't work well
since, once cut, the potatoes don't hold together well
enough for grating.

Hungarian pork with peppers

Serves 8

620 calories per serving

Takes 20 minutes to prepare,
15 minutes to cook

8 x 150 g (5½ oz) lean pork
chops, trimmed of visible fat

4 teaspoons smoked paprika

calorie controlled cooking
spray

4 onions, sliced

4 garlic cloves, sliced

4 green peppers, de-seeded
and sliced

500 ml (18 fl oz) chicken stock

400 g (14 oz) dried brown rice

225 g (8 oz) frozen peas

salt and freshly ground black
pepper

*The smoked paprika and green peppers give a Hungarian
flavour to this braised pork dish.*

1 Season the chops on both sides and dust with the paprika.
Spray a large, lidded, non stick frying pan (see Tip) with the
cooking spray and heat until hot. Add the chops and cook for
5 minutes, turning until golden. You may have to do this in
batches. Remove from the pan and set aside.

2 Re-spray the pan with the cooking spray and add the onions,
garlic and peppers. Stir-fry for 3–4 minutes until beginning to
soften. Reduce the heat, add the stock and return the chops
to the pan on top of the peppers and onions. Bring to the boil,
reduce to a simmer, cover and cook for 15 minutes until the
chops are cooked through.

3 Meanwhile, bring a large pan of water to the boil, add the
rice and cook according to the packet instructions. Add the
peas for the last 2 minutes of the cooking time. Drain well.

4 Serve the chops on top of the rice and peas with the
peppers, onions and juices.

Tip... If you don't have a large, lidded, non stick frying
pan, use a baking tray to cover your pan, making sure you
check the liquid doesn't evaporate too much.

Fantastic fish and seafood

Baked prawn risotto

Serves 4

292 calories per serving

Takes 10 minutes to prepare,
30 minutes to cook

calorie controlled cooking
spray

1 onion, chopped finely

2 garlic cloves, chopped

200 g (7 oz) dried risotto rice

75 ml (3 fl oz) dry Martini

50 ml (2 fl oz) Pernod

600 ml (20 fl oz) hot fish stock

200 g (7 oz) peeled raw king
prawns, defrosted if frozen

100 g (3½ oz) peeled cooked
prawns, defrosted if frozen

½ x 290 g jar marinated
artichoke antipasti, drained
and quartered

grated zest of a lemon

2 tablespoons finely chopped
fresh curly parsley

salt and freshly ground black
pepper

This stress-free risotto is so easy.

1 Preheat the oven to Gas Mark 4/180°C/fan oven 160°C.
Heat a non stick frying pan and spray with the cooking
spray. Cook the onion for 3–4 minutes until softened but not
coloured. Add the garlic and cook for 1 minute. Stir in the rice,
pour in the Martini and Pernod and allow it all to bubble for
30–60 seconds. Transfer the mixture to a non stick roasting
pan and pour in the fish stock.

2 Bake in the oven for 20–25 minutes until nearly tender and
the juices have been absorbed. Remove from the oven and stir
in the king prawns, cooked prawns, artichoke hearts and lemon
zest. Season.

3 Cook in the oven for a further 5 minutes until all the prawns
are cooked through. Check the seasoning, stir through the
parsley and serve immediately.

Tuna cakes with spring onion salsa

Serves 4

128 calories per serving

Takes 35 minutes

400 g (14 oz) potatoes, peeled and diced

185 g can tuna chunks in brine or spring water, drained and flaked roughly

1 teaspoon lemon juice

1 teaspoon olive oil

salt and freshly ground black pepper

For the salsa

4 spring onions, chopped finely

5 cm (2 inches) cucumber, de-seeded and diced finely

1 teaspoon lemon juice

Serve these tasty tuna cakes with a fresh tomato salad.

1 Bring a pan of water to the boil, add the potatoes and cook for 15–20 minutes until tender.

2 Meanwhile, in a small bowl mix together all the salsa ingredients. Set aside to marinate.

3 When the potatoes are just cooked through, drain and mash them. Stir in the tuna and lemon juice and season to taste. Using wet hands, divide the mixture into eight and shape into small cakes.

4 Heat the oil in a large non stick frying pan and fry the cakes for 3 minutes. Gently turn them over and cook for a further 2 minutes until golden brown.

5 Serve two tuna cakes per person with a helping of salsa.

Roast salmon fillets with tangy tomato crust

Serves 4
380 calories per serving
Takes 35 minutes

These crisp, tangy fillets are an easy midweek supper.
Serve with steamed broccoli.

1 Preheat the oven to Gas Mark 6/200°C/fan oven 180°C.

2 egg whites

1 tablespoon tomato purée

4 x 150 g (5½ oz) skinless salmon fillets

100 g (3½ oz) fresh white breadcrumbs

calorie controlled cooking spray

200 g (7 oz) cherry tomatoes, halved

a large bunch of fresh basil or coriander, chopped (optional)

1 teaspoon balsamic vinegar

salt and freshly ground black pepper

2 Beat the egg whites with the tomato purée and seasoning. Dip the fish fillets in the egg mixture first and then in the breadcrumbs to coat.

3 Place the coated fish on a non stick baking tray sprayed with the cooking spray and bake for 25 minutes.

4 Meanwhile, place the cherry tomatoes, basil or coriander, if using, balsamic vinegar and seasoning in a small saucepan with 50 ml (2 fl oz) of warm water and cook over a low heat, stirring, until the tomatoes start to break down.

5 Serve the fish with the cherry tomatoes spooned over.

Smoked mackerel hotpots

Serves 4
400 calories per serving
Takes 20 minutes

1 teaspoon vegetable oil
1 small onion, chopped finely
2 celery sticks, chopped
1 courgette, chopped
350 g (12 oz) smoked mackerel fillets, skinned and flaked
4 tomatoes, de-seeded and chopped
juice of ¼ of a lemon
4 tablespoons low fat soft cheese
25 g (1 oz) fresh white breadcrumbs
25 g (1 oz) half fat Cheddar cheese, grated
salt and freshly ground black pepper

Make these in individual ramekins – there is something special about having your very own portion. Serve with baby new potatoes and peas.

1 Heat the oil in a non stick saucepan and fry the onion, celery and courgette for 5 minutes. Remove from the heat and stir in the flaked mackerel and tomatoes.

2 Mix together the lemon juice and soft cheese. Season and fold into the smoked mackerel.

3 Either divide the mixture between four 10 cm (4 inch) ramekins or spoon into an 850 ml (1½ pint) shallow flameproof dish. Preheat the grill to medium.

4 Mix together the breadcrumbs and cheese and spread evenly over the surface of the mackerel mixture.

5 Grill for 4–5 minutes, or until the crumbs are golden and the cheese is bubbling.

Oriental-style fish parcels

Serves 2
181 calories per serving
Takes 25 minutes

2 x 150 g (5½ oz) skinless cod fillets
6 thick slices fresh root ginger
½ red pepper, de-seeded and cut into strips
1 carrot, peeled and sliced into ribbons
1 courgette, sliced into ribbons
2 spring onions, sliced into strips lengthways
1 tablespoon soy sauce
½ teaspoon sesame oil
4 teaspoons orange juice
freshly ground black pepper

Cooking food in a parcel helps to retain moisture. For a complete meal, serve with vegetables such as steamed spinach and 60 g (2 oz) dried brown rice per person, cooked according to the packet instructions.

1 Preheat the oven to Gas Mark 6/200°C/fan oven 180°C. Place each piece of fish on a large sheet of foil or non stick baking parchment. Top with the ginger, pepper, carrot, courgette and spring onions, divided equally.

2 In a bowl, mix together the soy sauce, sesame oil and orange juice and spoon over the fish. Season with black pepper and fold up the edges of the foil or baking parchment to make two loose parcels.

3 Place the parcels on a baking tray and bake for 15 minutes. Carefully open up one parcel to make sure the fish is cooked and then serve.

Sweet chilli fish

Serves 4
380 calories per serving
Takes 35 minutes

calorie controlled cooking spray

4 x 100 g (3½ oz) salmon fillets

a small bunch of fresh coriander or mint, to garnish (optional)

For the sweet chilli glaze

1 teaspoon dried chilli flakes

2 tablespoons light brown soft sugar

2 teaspoons soy sauce

juice of a lemon

½ teaspoon ground allspice

For the mixed beans

2 garlic cloves, chopped

2 teaspoons cumin seeds

1 large red pepper, de-seeded and chopped finely

1 tablespoon paprika

2 x 400 g cans mixed beans, drained and rinsed

4 tablespoons virtually fat free plain fromage frais

Salmon fillets are perfectly complemented by the sweet chilli glaze and bed of creamy beans.

1 Put all the sweet chilli glaze ingredients in a small pan and gently bring to the boil. Simmer for 5 minutes until thickened and then remove from the heat.

2 Meanwhile, heat a large, lidded, non stick frying pan and spray with the cooking spray. Stir-fry the garlic, cumin seeds and red pepper for 4 minutes until turning golden.

3 Add the paprika, beans and fromage frais and gently warm through for 2 minutes. Turn off the heat, cover and leave while you grill the fish.

4 Preheat the grill to hot and place a piece of foil on the grill pan. Spray with the cooking spray and place the salmon fillets on the foil, skin side up. Grill for 2 minutes on each side. Brush with the chilli glaze and grill for 1 minute more on each side until the glaze begins to burn. (Watch carefully as this happens very quickly.)

5 Spoon the beans on to serving plates, top with the salmon and serve garnished with the coriander or mint, if using.

Variation... Try canned lentils instead of the mixed beans.

Crab and asparagus fettuccine

Serves 2
415 calories per serving
Takes 15 minutes

200 g can white crab meat, drained
½ teaspoon dried chilli flakes
1 teaspoon lemon juice
175 g (6 oz) dried fettuccine
150 g (5½ oz) asparagus tips
salt and freshly ground black pepper

This is a lovely light but filling dish for the summer months.

1 Place the drained crab meat, chilli flakes and lemon juice in a bowl and mix them together thoroughly.

2 Bring a pan of water to the boil, add the pasta and cook for about 10 minutes until tender or according to the packet instructions. Add the asparagus to the pan for the last 2 minutes of the cooking time.

3 Drain the fettuccine and asparagus well, reserving 3 tablespoons of the cooking water. Return it all to a clean pan with the crab mixture. Heat through gently and season to taste. Serve at once.

Variation... Try using 200 g (7 oz) canned tuna in brine, drained and flaked, instead of the crab.

Goan fish curry

Serves 4
229 calories per serving
Takes 35 minutes
❄

calorie controlled cooking spray

2 onions, grated

2 long green chillies, de-seeded and sliced thinly

2 garlic cloves, chopped finely

4 cm (1½ inches) fresh root ginger, grated

2 teaspoons ground cumin

2 teaspoons turmeric

2 teaspoons garam masala

2 teaspoons ground coriander

3 cardamom pods, split

2 bay leaves

150 ml (5 fl oz) reduced fat coconut milk

400 g can chopped tomatoes

600 g (1 lb 5 oz) skinless haddock fillets, cut into chunks

juice of ½ a lime

salt and freshly ground black pepper

2 tablespoons chopped fresh coriander, to serve

Although there are quite a few ingredients in this dish, it really is simple. Serve with 60 g (2 oz) dried basmati rice per person, cooked according to the packet instructions.

1 Spray a large, lidded, non stick saucepan with the cooking spray and fry the onions over a medium heat, stirring frequently, for 7 minutes until softened and beginning to colour. Stir in the chillies, garlic, ginger, spices, cardamom pods and bay leaves and cook for 1 minute.

2 Pour in the coconut milk, tomatoes and 5 tablespoons of water and bring to the boil. Reduce the heat and simmer, half covered, for 5 minutes.

3 Add the haddock and continue to simmer, half covered, stirring occasionally and taking care not to break up the pieces of fish, for 10 minutes until the sauce has reduced and thickened.

4 Season to taste and stir in the lime juice. Serve sprinkled with the coriander.

Mussels in white wine

Serves 4
120 calories per serving
Takes 15 minutes to prepare,
  15 minutes to cook

1 tablespoon olive oil
1 small onion, chopped finely
2 garlic cloves, chopped finely
150 ml (5 fl oz) dry white wine
1¼ tomatoes, skinned and
  chopped
150 ml (5 fl oz) fish or
  vegetable stock
900 g (2 lb) mussels, prepared
  (see Tip)
freshly ground black pepper
2 tablespoons chopped fresh
  parsley or chives, to garnish

Farmed mussels are available all year round – so why not make use of them more often? Serve with a 50 g (1¾ oz) slice of crusty French bread to mop up the delicious juices.

1 Heat the olive oil in a very large, lidded, non stick saucepan. Add the onion and garlic and sauté until softened – about 3 minutes. Add the wine and tomatoes and heat until bubbling. Add the fish or vegetable stock and allow to boil for a few minutes to reduce and concentrate the liquid.

2 Tip the mussels into the saucepan. Cover and cook for 3–4 minutes, until the shells have opened. Season with black pepper and discard any mussels that remain shut.

3 Serve the mussels with the wine liquid and garnished with the parsley or chives.

Tip... To prepare mussels, scrub off any dirt and remove any barnacles. Remove the beard, if any, that sticks out between the shells. Discard any mussels that are already open or have a cracked shell.

Variation... For Thai-style mussels, add 1–2 teaspoons of Thai red or green curry paste with the stock and use chopped fresh coriander instead of parsley or chives.

Chinese prawns

Serves 2
353 calories per serving
Takes 25 minutes

150 g (5½ oz) dried basmati rice
calorie controlled cooking spray
200 g (7 oz) baby leeks
150 ml (5 fl oz) chicken stock
2 teaspoons grated or finely chopped fresh root ginger
1 tablespoon sherry vinegar or red wine vinegar
1 tablespoon soy sauce
175 g (6 oz) raw peeled prawns, defrosted if frozen
75 g (2¾ oz) spinach, washed

This will be on the table in less time than it takes to go for a take-away, and it tastes wonderful.

1 Bring a pan of water to the boil, add the rice and cook for 20 minutes or according to the packet instructions.

2 About 10 minutes before the rice will be ready, spray a wok or large non stick frying pan with the cooking spray and heat to a medium heat. Once hot, stir-fry the baby leeks for 2–3 minutes until browned and softened.

3 Turn the heat down to low and add the stock, ginger, vinegar and soy sauce. Simmer for another 2–3 minutes.

4 Add the prawns and cook them for 2–3 minutes or until they have changed to a pink colour all over.

5 Meanwhile, drain the rice and share between two plates. Add the spinach to the prawns and sauce, stir in until wilted and then serve immediately with the rice.

Variation... Use spring onions instead of the baby leeks or substitute pak choi or Chinese leaf lettuce for the spinach. Chinese leaf lettuce will take a little longer to cook, so add it when you add the prawns.

Salmon and dill fish pie

Serves 4
324 calories per serving
Takes 20 minutes
❄ (filling only, for up to
    1 month)

750 g (1 lb 10 oz) potatoes,
    peeled and chopped
325 g (11½ oz) salmon fillet
150 ml (5 fl oz) skimmed milk
calorie controlled cooking
    spray
175 g (6 oz) mushrooms,
    chopped
2 celery sticks, diced
100 g (3½ oz) spinach, washed
6 tablespoons virtually fat free
    plain fromage frais
3 tablespoons chopped fresh
    dill
salt and freshly ground black
    pepper

A tomato-based fish pie with sweet, fresh dill and
succulent salmon. Serve with a crisp green salad.

1 Preheat the oven to Gas Mark 6/200°C/fan oven 180°C.

2 Bring a pan of water to the boil, add the potatoes and cook
until tender.

3 Meanwhile, place the salmon and milk in a small pan and
simmer for 4–5 minutes until the salmon is just cooked. Drain,
reserving the milk. Flake the salmon into big chunks, removing
the skin and any bones.

4 Heat a large, lidded, non stick pan, spray with the
cooking spray, add the mushrooms and celery and cook for
4–5 minutes. Stir in the spinach, cover and cook for another
2–3 minutes until the spinach has wilted.

5 Add the salmon and fromage frais, stir well to combine
and simmer for 1–2 minutes before stirring in the dill and
seasoning. Pour into a shallow ovenproof dish.

6 Drain the potatoes and mash with 100 ml (3½ fl oz) of the
milk that was used to cook the salmon. Season well and spoon
over the salmon.

7 Place in the oven and cook for 10 minutes until the potato
topping is bubbling and golden.

Macaroni cheese and tuna bake

Serves 4

425 calories per serving

Takes 30 minutes to prepare,
20 minutes to cook

❄

25 g (1 oz) low fat spread

25 g (1 oz) plain white flour

300 ml (10 fl oz) skimmed milk

150 g (5½ oz) low fat soft
cheese with garlic and herbs

100 g (3½ oz) frozen peas

100 g (3½ oz) frozen
sweetcorn

1 red pepper, de-seeded and
diced

200 g (7 oz) canned tuna in
brine, drained and flaked

225 g (8 oz) dried quick-cook
macaroni

2 tomatoes, sliced

1 teaspoon dried oregano

salt and freshly ground black
pepper

A great midweek meal that all the family will enjoy.

1 Preheat the oven to Gas Mark 5/190°C/fan oven 170°C.

2 Gently heat the low fat spread in a small heavy based saucepan and stir in the flour. Gradually add the milk, whisking until you have a smooth, thickened sauce. Remove from the heat and stir in the soft cheese. Add in the peas, sweetcorn, red pepper, tuna and seasoning.

3 Meanwhile, bring a pan of water to the boil, add the pasta and cook according to the packet instructions. Drain thoroughly and fold it into the tuna sauce.

4 Transfer the macaroni to an ovenproof dish and arrange the tomato slices on top. Sprinkle over the oregano and bake for 20 minutes.

Tip... Take care when making a sauce with low fat spread – you will need to whisk it continuously while adding the milk as it easily turns lumpy. If it starts getting a little lumpy, remove the pan from the heat and whisk the sauce vigorously for a few seconds with an electric beater or a balloon whisk.

Baked trout with lemon and parsley pesto

Serves 2
450 calories per serving
Takes 15 minutes to prepare,
  20 minutes to cook
❄ (pesto only)

2 x 350 g (12 oz) whole trout
  (not rainbow trout), cleaned
  and gutted
2 large parsley sprigs
1 tablespoon dry white wine
salt and freshly ground black
  pepper
lemon wedges, to serve

For the pesto
1 garlic clove, chopped
25 g (1 oz) fresh parsley,
  chopped roughly
1 tablespoon olive oil
2 anchovy fillets
finely grated zest of a lemon
1 tablespoon lemon juice
1 tablespoon pine nut kernels

*Ask your fishmonger to prepare the trout for you; if buying
from a supermarket, they are normally ready-cleaned.
Serve with a green salad.*

1 Preheat the oven to Gas Mark 5/190°C/fan oven 170°C.
Line a shallow roasting tin with non stick baking parchment.

2 Rinse the fish and pat dry with kitchen towel. Season the
cavities and insert a parsley sprig into each one. Lift into the
roasting tin and drizzle with the wine. Bake for 20 minutes.

3 Meanwhile, to make the pesto, place all the ingredients in a
food processor. Blend until well chopped and evenly combined.
Transfer to a small bowl and season to taste.

4 Serve the baked trout with a spoonful of the lemon and
parsley pesto and lemon wedges to squeeze over.

Seafood kebabs with a chilli lime glaze

Serves 4
235 calories per serving
Takes 15 minutes

450 g (1 lb) skinless cod fillet, cut into 2.5 cm (1 inch) chunks

300 g (10½ oz) skinless salmon fillet, cut into 2.5 cm (1 inch) chunks

1 garlic clove, crushed, or 1 teaspoon garlic purée

2 teaspoons hot chilli paste

juice of ½ a lime

8 cherry tomatoes or 4 small tomatoes, halved

1 lime, cut into quarters

a handful of chopped fresh coriander, to garnish

Succulent and meaty, cod and salmon are a popular choice. Serve with 60 g (2 oz) dried long grain rice per person, cooked according to the packet instructions, with a pinch of turmeric for colour, and salad or green beans.

1 Place the fish in a plastic bag. Mix together the garlic, chilli paste and lime juice, add to the fish, twist the bag to seal, and gently shake to coat the fish with the marinade.

2 Divide the fish, tomatoes and lime wedges into four groups and then thread each group on to one of four skewers. Preheat the grill to high and place a piece of foil on the grill rack.

3 Use any remaining glaze to brush the kebabs and then grill for 3–4 minutes on each side, or until the fish becomes opaque. Serve garnished with the coriander.

Tip... If using wooden skewers, soak them in water for 30 minutes beforehand to prevent them from burning.

Variation... For a special occasion, replace some or all of the cod with 225 g (8 oz) each of scallops and peeled raw tiger prawns.

Quick sardine penne

Serves 2
330 calories per serving
Takes 20 minutes

125 g (4½ oz) dried penne
150 g (5½ oz) canned sardines
  in tomato sauce
1 tablespoon lemon juice
2 tablespoons torn fresh basil
salt and freshly ground black
  pepper

This is a super supper dish for when you are hungry but in a hurry.

1 Bring a pan of water to the boil, add the pasta and cook for about 10 minutes until tender or according to the packet instructions. Drain well.

2 Place the sardines and their tomato sauce in a bowl and mash with a fork. Stir in the lemon juice, basil and seasoning.

3 Return the pasta to a large saucepan. Add the sardine mixture, heat through for 2–3 minutes and serve hot.

Variation... Try this dish with 150 g (5½ oz) canned pilchards instead of the sardines.

Fish crumble

Serves 4
278 calories per serving
Takes 20 minutes to prepare,
40 minutes to cook
❄

300 g (10½ oz) skinless smoked haddock fillet, cut into bite size pieces
100 ml (3½ fl oz) skimmed milk
415 g can reduced sugar and salt baked beans
75 g (2¾ oz) frozen peas

For the crumble topping
50 g (1¾ oz) plain wholemeal flour
40 g (1½ oz) low fat spread
50 g (1¾ oz) porridge oats
2 teaspoons dried mixed herbs
salt and freshly ground black pepper

Baked beans add a touch of sweetness and their tomato sauce goes well with the fish and peas. Make double the topping and freeze for later. Serve with steamed broccoli.

1 Preheat the oven to Gas Mark 5/190°C/fan oven 170°C. Place the fish in the bottom of an ovenproof dish.

2 Put the milk, beans and peas in a saucepan and heat for 3–4 minutes until the peas have defrosted and the mixture is hot. Pour over the fish.

3 To make the crumble topping, place the flour in a large bowl, add the low fat spread and rub it in using your fingertips until it resembles breadcrumbs. Stir in the oats and herbs with a little seasoning.

4 Sprinkle over the fish and bake for 40 minutes until golden and hot.

Quick prawn and crab noodles

Serves 4
440 calories per serving
Takes 25 minutes

1 tablespoon tomato purée
1 tablespoon light soy sauce
1 tablespoon cider or light malt vinegar
1 tablespoon dark or light muscovado sugar
2 teaspoons cornflour
225 g (8 oz) dried thread egg noodles
2 teaspoons stir-fry oil or vegetable oil
1 red pepper, de-seeded and sliced finely
a bunch of spring onions, sliced finely
1 courgette, sliced
100 g (3½ oz) mange tout, sliced
225 g (8 oz) large, cooked, peeled prawns, defrosted if frozen
8 crab sticks, defrosted if frozen, chopped into chunks
salt and freshly ground black pepper

Prawns and crab sticks make a quick meal when combined with instant egg noodles and a few vegetables.

1 In a small bowl, mix together the tomato purée, soy sauce, vinegar, sugar and cornflour. Set aside.

2 Bring a pan of water to the boil, add the noodles and cook for about 6 minutes or according to the packet instructions.

3 Meanwhile, heat the oil in a wok or large non stick frying pan. Add the pepper, spring onions, courgette and mange tout and stir-fry over a high heat for 3–4 minutes.

4 Add the prawns and crab sticks and cook, stirring, for 2 minutes until hot. Stir the soy sauce mixture, add to the wok or frying pan and cook, stirring constantly, until thickened and blended. Season to taste.

5 Drain the noodles and divide between four warmed serving bowls. Pile the prawn mixture on top and serve at once.

Tip... Muscovado sugar gives a lovely flavour to the sweet and sour sauce in this recipe; it doesn't really matter whether you use the dark or light variety. If you haven't got any to hand, you could use ordinary brown sugar, although the flavour will not be quite as nice.

Simply vegetarian

Tofu kebabs with peanut sauce

Serves 2

220 calories per serving

Takes 15 minutes to prepare,
15 minutes to cook

200 g (7 oz) tofu, cut into bite
size squares

2 tablespoons light soy sauce

1 teaspoon sesame oil

1 large garlic clove, crushed

1 red or yellow pepper,
de-seeded and cut into bite
size squares

1 Little Gem lettuce, shredded,
to serve

For the sauce

1 spring onion, chopped finely

¼ teaspoon chilli powder

½ teaspoon caster sugar

2 teaspoons white wine
vinegar

1 tablespoon crunchy peanut
butter

*Treat yourself to an exotic Thai-style main meal, served
with a luxurious peanut sauce.*

1 Mix the tofu together with 1 tablespoon of soy sauce, the
sesame oil and garlic. Leave it to marinate for 5 minutes.

2 Thread the tofu and pepper pieces alternately on to wooden
satay sticks.

3 In a small saucepan, heat the sauce ingredients together
with the remaining soy sauce for 2–3 minutes until just hot and
blended together. Preheat the grill to high.

4 Grill the tofu kebabs for about 5–6 minutes, turning them
once, until they are crispy. Serve the kebabs on the shredded
lettuce, with the sauce spooned over.

Tip... Soak the satay sticks in water for 30 minutes
beforehand to prevent them from burning.

Baked feta and tomato marrow

Serves 4

230 calories per serving

Takes 15 minutes to prepare, 30 minutes to cook ✔ ❄ (tomato sauce only)

Try this delicious recipe – served with a robust tomato and herb sauce – accompanied by fresh green beans.

For the tomato sauce
400 g can chopped tomatoes
1 small onion, chopped finely
1 celery stick, chopped finely
1 small carrot, peeled and chopped finely
½ garlic clove, chopped
a small bunch of fresh parsley, chopped
1 teaspoon caster sugar
2 teaspoons chopped fresh thyme or ½ teaspoon dried thyme
salt and freshly ground black pepper

For the marrow
675 g (1½ lb) marrow, peeled, de-seeded and cut into 5 cm (1 inch) rings
1 onion, chopped finely
1 tablespoon vegetable oil
1 garlic clove, chopped
175 g (6 oz) mushrooms, chopped roughly
175 g (6 oz) cooked long grain rice
1 teaspoon chopped fresh rosemary or ½ teaspoon dried rosemary
100 g (3½ oz) feta cheese, crumbled

1 Put all the ingredients for the tomato sauce in a heavy based lidded saucepan, cover and simmer over a gentle heat for 30 minutes. Whizz to a smooth sauce using a blender or hand blender and return to the pan. Adjust the seasoning to taste. If the sauce is too thin, reduce by boiling rapidly. Keep warm.

2 Meanwhile, bring a pan of water to the boil, add the marrow and cook for 3–4 minutes, or until tender. Drain thoroughly, drying on kitchen towel, and then arrange in a shallow ovenproof dish.

continues opposite ▶

▶ *Baked feta and tomato marrow* continued

3 Preheat the oven to Gas Mark 6/200°C/fan oven 180°C.

4 Heat a non stick frying pan and cook the onion in the oil until soft. Add the garlic and cook for a further minute before stirring in the mushrooms. Increase the heat and stir-fry the mushrooms, evaporating off any liquid released.

5 Stir in the rice and rosemary. Divide between the marrow rings and sprinkle over the feta cheese. Bake in the oven for 12–15 minutes, or until piping hot and golden brown. Serve immediately with the tomato sauce.

Variations... For a seafood version, replace the feta cheese with 175 g (6 oz) cooked peeled prawns, chopped and added with the rice.

For a non-vegetarian option, add a dash of Worcestershire sauce.

Pesto pasta with halloumi cheese

Serves 2

395 calories per serving

Takes 5 minutes to prepare,
  15 minutes to cook

**90 g (3¼ oz) dried pasta
  shapes**

**calorie controlled cooking
  spray**

**80 g (3 oz) halloumi cheese,
  sliced into rectangular
  fingers**

**a bunch of spring onions,
  chopped**

**1 large red pepper, de-seeded
  and sliced**

150 g (5½ oz) mange tout

**1 tablespoon red or green
  pesto**

**salt and freshly ground black
  pepper**

**a few fresh basil leaves, to
  garnish**

*You can use whatever pasta shapes you have to hand for
this delicious recipe – shells work well as they catch the
pesto sauce.*

1 Bring a pan of water to the boil, add the pasta and cook for
10–12 minutes, or according to the packet instructions. Drain
the pasta, reserving 4 tablespoons of the cooking liquid.

2 Meanwhile, put a large non stick frying pan on a medium
heat and spray with the cooking spray. Brown the halloumi by
gently frying it for 1–2 minutes on each side. Remove from the
frying pan and set aside on a warm plate.

3 Spray the frying pan again, add the spring onions and
pepper and stir-fry for a couple of minutes. Add the mange tout
and continue to cook for 3–5 minutes or until they are cooked
to your taste.

4 Add the reserved pasta cooking liquid to the frying pan and
stir in the pesto. Add the cooked pasta, mix thoroughly and
season to taste. Transfer the stir-fry to two warmed plates and
top with the halloumi and basil. Serve immediately.

Tip... Halloumi cheese doesn't melt, which makes it ideal
for kebabs and stir-fries. The fresher it is, the better it
stays together in the pan, so always look for the cheese
with the longest sell by date.

Sicilian stuffed peppers

Serves 4

365 calories per serving

Takes 15 minutes to prepare,
  20 minutes to cook

**4 red or yellow peppers,
  halved lengthways and
  de-seeded**

For the filling

**a small bunch of fresh parsley,
  chopped finely**

**a small bunch of fresh
  oregano, chopped finely**

**2 tablespoons capers, drained,
  dried and chopped**

1 garlic clove, crushed

**200 g (7 oz) fresh white
  breadcrumbs**

**4 ripe tomatoes, skinned,
  de-seeded and diced finely
  (see Tip)**

2 tablespoons currants

**20 stoned black olives in
  brine, drained and chopped**

**50 g (1¾ oz) toasted pine nut
  kernels**

**grated zest and juice of a
  lemon**

**salt and freshly ground black
  pepper**

These are delicious served with 60 g (2 oz) dried rice per person, cooked according to the packet instructions, and a crunchy salad.

1 Preheat the oven to Gas Mark 6/200°C/fan oven 180°C. Place the peppers cut side up on a non stick baking tray.

2 Mix all the filling ingredients together in a bowl and use to fill the pepper halves. Bake for 20 minutes until tender and golden on top and then serve.

Tip... To skin tomatoes easily, put the tomatoes in a bowl and cover with boiling water. Leave for about 10 seconds and then remove with a slotted spoon. Cool under cold water and the skin should peel off easily. If it doesn't, then return the tomatoes to the hot water for about 5 seconds and try to peel them again. This method of preparation is also perfect for preparing tomatoes for including in salsas.

Variations... Large beef or plum tomatoes or courgettes can be stuffed with the same mixture.

For a non-vegetarian version, add 6 drained and chopped canned anchovy fillets to the filling mixture.

Leeks and beans with cheese sauce

Serves 2
215 calories per serving
Takes 20 minutes

10 baby leeks, trimmed, or
   2 leeks, sliced thickly
300 g (10½ oz) canned
   cannellini beans, drained
   and rinsed
2 teaspoons cornflour
75 g (2¾ oz) low fat soft
   cheese with garlic and herbs
2 tablespoons chopped fresh
   chives
2 teaspoons grated Parmesan
   cheese
salt and freshly ground black
   pepper

Tasty grilled cheese on top of creamy leeks and cannellini beans is so delicious. You can enjoy it piping hot, straight from the dish, and mop up the sauce with a medium slice of granary bread per person. Serve with a tomato and onion salad.

1 Bring a pan of water to the boil, add the leeks and cook for 5–7 minutes, until just tender. Drain thoroughly, reserving 150 ml (5 fl oz) of the cooking liquid. Arrange the leeks and cannellini beans in two shallow flameproof dishes.

2 Blend the cornflour with the cooking liquid and return to the pan. Bring to the boil, stirring, until smooth and thickened. Add the soft cheese and chives and season to taste. Simmer until the sauce is smooth. Preheat the grill to medium.

3 Pour the sauce over the leeks and beans and sprinkle with the Parmesan cheese. Place under the grill for 4–5 minutes until golden and bubbling.

Variations... Replace the leeks with asparagus, or use a mixture of the two.

For a non-vegetarian version, replace the beans with 150 g (5½ oz) wafer thin smoked ham.

Autumn quiche

Serves 6

187 calories per serving

Takes 30 minutes to prepare,
30 minutes to cook

350 g (12 oz) butternut
squash, peeled, de-seeded
and cut into 1.5 cm
(⅝ inch) chunks

200 g (7 oz) parsnip, peeled
and cut into 1.5 cm
(⅝ inch) chunks

175 g (6 oz) broccoli, cut into
small florets

½ x 290 g packet pizza base
mix

2 eggs, beaten

200 g (7 oz) low fat soft
cheese

1 teaspoon dried marjoram

salt and freshly ground black
pepper

Serve with a lamb's lettuce salad, drizzled with a little
fat free dressing, and a 50 g (1¾ oz) slice of French stick
per person.

1 Preheat the oven to Gas Mark 6/200°C/fan oven 180°C and
put a baking tray in the oven.

2 Put the butternut squash in a large lidded saucepan and
cover with cold water. Bring to the boil, cover and simmer for
5 minutes. Add the parsnip, cover again and simmer for a
further 3 minutes. Add the broccoli and simmer for 1 minute.
Drain thoroughly in a colander and pat the vegetables dry.

3 Meanwhile, empty the pizza base mix into a large bowl and
make it up according to the packet instructions. Put a piece
of non stick baking parchment on a clean surface and roll out
the dough on the paper into a circle at least 26 cm wide. Line
a 20 x 3 cm deep (8 x 1¼ inch) fluted flan tin with the circle
of dough, discarding the paper and trimming the edges of the
dough where needed.

4 Arrange the butternut squash, parsnip and broccoli over
the base of the quiche. In a jug, mix together the eggs, soft
cheese, marjoram and seasoning until smooth. Pour over the
vegetables, transfer to the preheated baking tray and bake in
the oven for 30 minutes until golden and just set. Leave in the
tin for 5 minutes before cutting into wedges and serving.

Quorn shepherd's pie

Serves 4
373 calories per serving
Takes 50 minutes

750g (1 lb 10 oz) potatoes, peeled and diced

4 parsnips, peeled and diced

calorie controlled cooking spray

2 carrots, peeled and diced finely

2 celery sticks, diced finely

2 onions, chopped finely

2 garlic cloves, crushed

300 g (10½ oz) Quorn mince

600 ml (20 fl oz) vegetable stock

400 g can chopped tomatoes

a dash of Tabasco sauce

4 tablespoons skimmed milk or soya milk

salt and freshly ground black pepper

This is a fabulous vegetarian version of the family favourite.

1 Bring a large pan of water to the boil, add the potatoes and parsnips and cook for 10–15 minutes until tender.

2 Meanwhile, heat a large non stick frying pan and spray with the cooking spray. Stir-fry the carrots, celery, onions and garlic for 5 minutes, until softened, adding a splash of water if necessary to prevent them from sticking.

3 Add the Quorn and stock, bring to the boil and simmer rapidly for 10 minutes. Add the tomatoes and Tabasco sauce and simmer a further 10 minutes until thick. Check the seasoning.

4 Preheat the grill to high, drain the potatoes and parsnips and mash with the milk and some seasoning.

5 Spoon the Quorn mixture into an ovenproof dish. Top with the mash and grill for 2 minutes until bubbling and golden.

Vegetable jalfrezi

Serves 4
341 calories per serving
Takes 20 minutes to prepare, 30 minutes to cook ❤ ❄

Ready-made curry pastes make it easy to cook your own rather than order a take-away.

calorie controlled cooking spray
1 large onion, chopped
1 eating apple, cored and chopped
1 garlic clove, crushed
3 tablespoons jalfrezi curry paste
2 carrots, peeled and sliced
1 red pepper, de-seeded and chopped
400 g can chopped tomatoes
175 g (6 oz) cauliflower or broccoli, broken into florets

410 g can chick peas, drained and rinsed
300 ml (10 fl oz) vegetable stock
50 g (1¾ oz) frozen peas
2 tablespoons chopped fresh coriander
salt and freshly ground black pepper

To serve
4 plain Weight Watchers mini naan breads
4 tablespoons low fat natural yogurt

1 Heat a large lidded saucepan and spray with the cooking spray. Add the onion, apple and garlic and stir-fry for 2 minutes. Add the curry paste and cook for a few seconds more.

2 Add the carrots, pepper, tomatoes, cauliflower or broccoli, chick peas and stock. Simmer, partially covered, for 25–30 minutes, adding a little extra stock or water if it seems to be getting too dry.

3 Add the peas and coriander and heat for a few moments. Check the seasoning. Preheat the grill.

4 Warm the bread under the grill for a couple of minutes. Serve the curry on warmed plates with 1 tablespoon of yogurt each and a naan bread.

Variation... Try using 400 g (14 oz) potatoes, cut into small chunks, instead of the chick peas.

Gougère with mushroom filling

Serves 6

250 calories per serving

Takes 20 minutes to prepare,
40 minutes to cook

**calorie controlled cooking
spray**

100 g (3½ oz) plain white flour

75 g (2¾ oz) low fat spread

3 eggs, beaten lightly

**50 g (1¾ oz) Gruyère cheese,
cut into 5 mm (¼ inch) dice,
plus 15 g (½ oz) grated finely**

**salt and freshly ground black
pepper**

For the filling

**750 g (1 lb 10 oz) open cup
mushrooms, chopped
roughly**

3 garlic cloves, crushed

**75 g (2¾ oz) stoned black
olives in brine, drained and
sliced**

**2 teaspoons dried herbes de
Provence or dried mixed
herbs**

**200 g (7 oz) cherry tomatoes,
quartered**

*A gougère is a savoury choux pastry case baked with a
filling.*

1 Preheat the oven to Gas Mark 6/200°C/fan oven 180°C.
Spray a large ovenproof baking dish with the cooking spray.
Fold a piece of baking parchment or foil in half, open out and
sift on the flour and a pinch of salt. Add a little black pepper.

2 Place the low fat spread in a non stick saucepan with
200 ml (7 fl oz) of cold water and bring to a rolling boil. Remove
from the heat and quickly tip in the flour. Stir briskly until the
mixture comes together as a ball. Sit the pan in a basin of cold
water for about 10 minutes or until the dough is cool.

3 Gradually mix the beaten eggs into the dough until you have
a smooth and shiny batter that drops easily from the spoon. Stir
in the diced cheese and then dollop spoonfuls around the edge
of the baking dish, just touching each other, leaving a hole in
the centre for the filling. Bake for 25 minutes.

4 Meanwhile, for the filling, place the mushrooms, garlic
and 2 tablespoons of water in a large lidded saucepan. Cook,
covered, for 5 minutes until the mushrooms release their
juices. Remove the lid and continue cooking until the juices
have evaporated.

5 Stir the olives and herbs in with the mushrooms and cook,
uncovered, for 10 minutes. Spoon the filling into the centre of
the gougère, scatter the tomatoes over the top and sprinkle the
grated cheese over the risen pastry case. Bake for 15 minutes
and serve immediately.

Spanish vegetable rice

Serves 4

313 calories per serving

Takes 15 minutes to prepare,
  20 minutes to cook

calorie controlled cooking
  spray

1 onion, chopped finely

1 red pepper, de-seeded and
  sliced

1 yellow pepper, de-seeded
  and sliced

200 g (7 oz) button
  mushrooms, halved

3 tomatoes, chopped roughly

250 g (9 oz) dried paella or
  risotto rice

850 ml (1½ pints) hot
  vegetable stock

a pinch of saffron strands
  (optional)

200 g (7 oz) frozen peas

juice of ½ a lemon

2 heaped tablespoons
  chopped fresh parsley

salt and freshly ground black
  pepper

*This is a tasty vegetarian version of the Spanish favourite,
paella.*

1 Place a large, lidded, non stick saucepan on the hob and
spray with the cooking spray. Add the onion with 2 tablespoons
of water and cook for 4 minutes. Stir in the peppers and cook
for a further 2 minutes.

2 Add the mushrooms and tomatoes and cook for 2 minutes
or until the tomatoes start to soften. Mix in the rice and cook,
stirring, for 1 minute.

3 Pour in 700 ml (1¼ pints) of the stock, add the saffron, if
using, and bring to the boil. Season, cover and simmer gently
for 15 minutes until the rice is almost tender and most of the
stock has been absorbed.

4 Add the peas and the remaining stock to the pan and cook,
uncovered, for 5 minutes. Stir in the lemon juice and parsley
just before serving.

Variation... For a non-vegetarian version, try stirring in
250 g (9 oz) cooked peeled prawns with the peas.

Spinach and ricotta cannelloni

Serves 2
199 calories per serving
Takes 30 minutes

2 sheets fresh lasagne,
    measuring 17 x 22 cm
    (6½ x 8½ inches)
150 g (5½ oz) frozen spinach,
    defrosted
110 g (4 oz) ricotta cheese
300 g (10½ oz) passata with
    herbs
salt and freshly ground black
    pepper
a handful of fresh basil leaves,
    torn, to garnish

This is a fast way to make a delicious cannelloni.

1 Preheat the oven to Gas Mark 6/200°C/fan oven 180°C.
Halve each lasagne sheet to create four rectangles
approximately 17 x 11 cm (6½ x 4 inches). Bring a large pan
of water to the boil, add the pasta and cook according to the
packet instructions. Drain and keep warm.

2 Mix together the spinach and ricotta and season. Place
2 tablespoons of the spinach mixture in a line in the centre of
a pasta rectangle and roll up. Repeat with the other rectangles
using all the mixture. Place the tubes in an ovenproof dish.

3 Pour the passata over the cannelloni. Bake for 15 minutes
until bubbling. Serve garnished with the fresh basil leaves.

Red pepper and pasta tortilla

Serves 4

210 calories per serving

Takes 10 minutes to prepare, 20 minutes to cook

50 g (1¾ oz) dried pasta shapes

1 tablespoon olive oil

a bunch of spring onions, sliced

1 garlic clove, crushed

1 red pepper, de-seeded and sliced

1 orange or yellow pepper, de-seeded and sliced

4 eggs

2 tablespoons skimmed milk

2 tablespoons chopped mixed fresh basil, chives or parsley

salt and freshly ground black pepper

a bag of mixed salad leaves, to serve

For a quick and easy meal, make this Spanish-style omelette with cooked pasta shapes, sliced peppers, spring onions and chopped fresh herbs.

1 Bring a pan of water to the boil, add the pasta and cook for about 8–10 minutes until just tender, or according to the packet instructions.

2 Meanwhile, heat the olive oil in a large non stick omelette pan with a flameproof handle and cook the spring onions, garlic and peppers for about 5 minutes, stirring often.

3 Drain the pasta thoroughly and add to the omelette pan. Beat the eggs and milk together, add the herbs, season and pour into the pan. Preheat the grill to medium.

4 Cook on the hob over a low heat until set on the base and then transfer to the grill and cook the top until set and brown.

5 Allow the tortilla to cool for a few minutes and then cut into quarters and serve with the salad leaves.

Variation... If you're not keen on peppers, substitute sliced mushrooms instead; you'll need about 175 g (6 oz).

Spring stew with gremolata

Serves 4
207 calories per serving
Takes 40 minutes ✓ ❄

Stew is turned into something special with the addition of gremolata – a herby condiment.

calorie controlled cooking spray
350 g (12 oz) baby onions, peeled
250 g (9 oz) baby turnips, peeled
300 g (10½ oz) baby carrots, scrubbed and trimmed
3 garlic cloves, chopped finely
1 teaspoon dried mixed herbs
2 bay leaves
150 ml (5 fl oz) dry white wine
250 ml (9 fl oz) vegetable stock

275 g (9½ oz) baby courgettes, cut into chunks
175 g (6 oz) frozen petit pois
salt and freshly ground black pepper

For the gremolata
2 slices white bread, crusts removed
1 tablespoon olive oil
grated zest and juice of a lemon
1 tablespoon chopped fresh parsley

1 Spray a large, lidded, non stick saucepan with the cooking spray. Add the onions and sauté, covered, for 4 minutes until they start to brown. Add the turnips, carrots, 2 garlic cloves, herbs and bay leaves and continue to cook, covered, for 3 minutes, stirring occasionally.

2 Pour in the wine, bring to the boil and cook until the wine has almost evaporated and the smell of alcohol has disappeared. Pour in the stock and simmer, uncovered, for 10 minutes, stirring occasionally.

3 Cover the pan, cook for another 5 minutes and then add the courgettes, peas and seasoning. Cook for a final 5 minutes.

4 Meanwhile, put the bread into a food processor and whizz until it forms breadcrumbs. Heat the oil in a frying pan and fry the breadcrumbs for 2 minutes until crisp and golden. Add the remaining garlic and fry for another 30 seconds. Finally, stir in the lemon zest, lemon juice and parsley.

5 Divide the vegetables between four warmed bowls and sprinkle with the gremolata.

Peppered Quorn stroganoff with mushroom sauce

Serves 4

155 calories per serving

Takes 25 minutes to prepare,
35 minutes to cook

❄

225 g (8 oz) Quorn Chicken
Style Pieces

1 vegetable stock cube,
crumbled

2 tablespoons boiling water

1 tablespoon olive oil

1 onion, sliced

1 garlic clove, crushed

225 g (8 oz) mushrooms,
sliced

300 g can reduced fat
mushroom soup

1 tablespoon brandy

3 tablespoons half fat crème
fraîche

salt and freshly ground black
pepper

Serve hot with 60 g (2 oz) dried basmati rice or pasta per person, cooked according to the packet instructions.

1 Place the Quorn in a bowl, sprinkle the stock cube over and add the boiling water. Stir well and leave to stand for 10 minutes.

2 Meanwhile, heat the olive oil in a pan and cook the onion, garlic and mushrooms until softened. Add the Quorn and cook for a further 2 minutes.

3 Stir in the soup, brandy and seasoning and simmer for 10 minutes.

4 Add the crème fraîche and heat through without boiling.

Mushrooms and shallots in red wine

Serves 2

127 calories per serving

Takes 5 minutes to prepare,
20 minutes to cook

Ⓥ

8 shallots, quartered

calorie controlled cooking
spray

2 large (or 4 medium)
portobello mushrooms

4 tablespoons balsamic
vinegar

150 ml (5 fl oz) red wine

150 ml (5 fl oz) vegetable
stock

salt and freshly ground black
pepper

*This is a wonderful vegetarian version of the recipe on
page 48.*

1 Bring a pan of water to the boil, add the shallots and simmer
for 2–3 minutes. Drain and set aside.

2 Spray a non stick frying pan with the cooking spray, season
the mushrooms and fry for 3–4 minutes on each side, or until
cooked through.

3 Remove the mushrooms to a plate and keep warm. Add
the shallots to the pan and stir-fry until browned. Add the
balsamic vinegar and allow to bubble briefly.

4 Add the wine and boil until the sauce is sticky. Add the stock
and simmer for a few minutes until thickened.

5 Spoon the shallots and sauce over the mushrooms and
serve immediately.

Watercress and blue cheese pasta

Serves 4

415 calories per serving

Takes 5 minutes to prepare,
10 minutes to cook

350 g (12 oz) dried pasta
shapes

50 g (1¾ oz) Danish blue
cheese

100 g (3½ oz) low fat soft
cheese

4 tablespoons skimmed milk

175 g (6 oz) watercress,
washed and chopped
roughly

salt and freshly ground black
pepper

*This recipe uses a little strong flavoured Danish blue
cheese, so you get all the flavour with less of the fat.*

1 Bring a pan of water to the boil, add the pasta and cook
according to the packet instructions. Drain.

2 Meanwhile, put the cheeses and milk in a large pan
and heat, gently stirring, until they are melted, smooth and
combined.

3 Toss the pasta with the sauce and watercress and season.

Pasta pomodoro

Serves 4

330 calories per serving

Takes 10 minutes to prepare,
15 minutes to cook

**225 g (8 oz) dried pasta
shapes**

1 tablespoon olive oil

1 onion, chopped finely

**100 g (3½ oz) mushrooms,
sliced**

400 g can chopped tomatoes

275 g jar tomato pasta sauce

**100 g (3½ oz) roasted pepper
strips in olive oil, drained
and rInsed**

**salt and freshly ground black
pepper**

**a handful of fresh basil leaves,
torn into pieces, to garnish**

*Use a ready-made pasta sauce with a few other
ingredients to make a quick and easy meal.*

1 Bring a pan of water to the boil, add the pasta and cook
for 8–10 minutes until tender, or according to the packet
instructions.

2 Meanwhile, heat the olive oil in a large non stick saucepan
and sauté the onion for about 3 minutes, until softened.

3 Add the mushrooms, tomatoes and pasta sauce. Bring to the
boil, reduce the heat and simmer for about 10 minutes.

4 Drain the pasta and add to the sauce with the pepper strips.
Season to taste and serve, garnished with the torn basil leaves.

Tip... Instead of using pepper strips in olive oil, buy a jar
of red peppers and slice the amount you need. Keep the
remainder in a covered container in the fridge and use
within 3 days.

Delicious desserts

Orange profiteroles with chocolate sauce

Serves 6
234 calories per serving
Takes 25 minutes to prepare + cooling, 25 minutes to bake ✓

Choux pastry is light and crisp and easy to make. The profiteroles are filled with orange flavoured sweetened ricotta cheese.

60 g (2 oz) plain white flour
40 g (1½ oz) low fat spread
1 egg
1 egg white

For the sauce
200 ml (7 fl oz) skimmed milk
100 g (3½ oz) dark chocolate (minimum 70% cocoa solids), chopped into small pieces

1 tablespoon golden syrup
grated zest of an orange

For the filling
150 g (5½ oz) ricotta cheese
2 teaspoons orange zest
1 tablespoon icing sugar, sifted

1 Preheat the oven to Gas Mark 6/200°C/fan oven 180°C. Line two baking trays with non stick baking parchment. Sift the flour on to a plate.

2 Place the low fat spread in a large pan with 125 ml (4 fl oz) of water. Bring to the boil and then remove from the heat. Add the flour and beat thoroughly until the mixture is smooth and forms a ball.

3 Whisk together the egg and egg white and then gradually beat the egg into the flour mixture. Make sure the mixture is beaten well to incorporate the air that makes the buns rise.

4 Use a teaspoon to place 18 dollops of the mixture on to the baking trays, leaving room for them to expand. Bake for 20 minutes until golden. Do not open the oven otherwise the profiteroles will sink.

continues overleaf ▶

5 Meanwhile, warm the milk in a small pan to just below boiling and then remove from the heat. Add the chocolate to the pan and stir to dissolve. If it doesn't quite dissolve, reheat very gently. Stir in the golden syrup and orange zest.

6 Remove the profiteroles from the oven and pierce each one with a skewer to let out the steam. Return to the oven for a further 5 minutes to dry out the insides. Transfer to a wire rack to cool completely.

7 To fill, mix the filling ingredients together, carefully slit the buns and spoon or pipe in the mixture. Serve three each, with the sauce.

Tips... Do not fill the buns more than 2 hours before serving otherwise they will go soggy. Try to make the buns fresh that day.

Make the sauce ahead of time and chill until required. It will set, so gently reheat in a pan or in the microwave.

Variation... For a mocha sauce, dissolve the chocolate in 100 ml (3½ fl oz) strong black coffee and then stir in 100 ml (3½ fl oz) skimmed milk.

Apricot surprise pudding

Serves 6

172 calories per serving

Takes 10 minutes to prepare + standing, 25 minutes to bake

calorie controlled cooking spray

3 eggs, separated

50 g (1¾ oz) caster sugar

50 g (1¾ oz) low fat spread

50 g (1¾ oz) self raising flour

grated zest of a large orange

100 ml (3½ fl oz) skimmed milk

411 g can apricot halves in natural juice, drained

15 g (½ oz) flaked toasted almonds

The surprise is that this pudding comes with its own zesty sauce at the bottom of the dish.

1 Preheat the oven to Gas Mark 4/180°C/fan oven 160°C and spray a 1.2 litre (2 pint) ovenproof dish with the cooking spray. In a large bowl, whisk together the egg yolks, sugar and low fat spread until pale and fluffy. Fold in the flour and orange zest and then gradually stir in the milk to make a smooth batter.

2 In a clean, grease-free bowl, whisk the egg whites until stiff peaks form. Fold the egg whites into the batter using a large metal spoon and then pour into the prepared dish. Put the dish in a deep roasting tin.

3 Carefully arrange the apricot halves, cut side down, in the batter and scatter over the almonds. Fill the roasting tin with cold water so that it comes halfway up the sides of the dish. Bake in the oven for 25 minutes until risen and firm on top. Leave to stand for 5 minutes and then serve immediately.

Banoffee pie

Serves 6
166 calories per serving
Takes 15 minutes +
   36 minutes chilling

40 g (1½ oz) low fat spread
135 g (4¾ oz) reduced fat
   digestive biscuits, crushed
calorie controlled cooking
   spray
1 butterscotch Angel Delight
   No Added Sugar
300 ml (10 fl oz) semi
   skimmed milk
2 bananas, chopped
200 ml (7 fl oz) low fat natural
   yogurt
3 teaspoons light muscovado
   sugar

A deliciously indulgent dessert.

1 Melt the low fat spread in a small saucepan, add the crushed biscuits and mix well.

2 Spray a 20 cm (8 inch) loose-bottomed flan tin with the cooking spray. Tip the crumb mixture into the tin and press it down well, right up to the edges. Chill in the fridge for 30 minutes.

3 Make up the butterscotch Angel Delight with the milk according to the packet instructions. After leaving for 2 minutes, spoon it over the biscuit base and return it to the fridge for 4 minutes or until set.

4 Top the pie with the chopped bananas and then the yogurt. Sprinkle with the sugar and return to the fridge for 2 minutes until the sugar starts to dissolve. Serve cut into six wedges.

Tip... The biscuit base can be made well in advance and then you can complete the dessert just before you require it.

Variation... Try using different flavours of Angel Delight with different fruits – try strawberry flavour, topped with 150 g (5½ oz) fresh sliced strawberries.

Cherry clafoutis

Serves 4

210 calories per serving

Takes 10 minutes to prepare,
25–30 minutes to cook

calorie controlled cooking
spray

110 g (4 oz) plain white flour

1 large egg

300 ml (10 fl oz) skimmed milk

1 tablespoon caster sugar

350 g (12 oz) cherries, stoned

**2 teaspoons icing sugar, for
dusting**

*This French-style hot dessert is wonderfully satisfying. It's
a lightly sweetened batter pudding with hot fresh cherries
– delicious.*

1 Preheat the oven to Gas Mark 6/200°C/fan oven 180°C.
Spray four individual ovenproof dishes with the cooking spray.

2 Put the flour, egg, milk and sugar into a large mixing bowl
and whisk together to make a smooth batter.

3 Divide the cherries between the dishes and pour an equal
amount of batter into each one. Transfer the dishes to the oven
and bake for 25–30 minutes, until set and golden.

4 Serve at once, dusted with the icing sugar.

Variation... When blackberries are in season, try using them
instead of cherries.

Chocolate fudge rice pudding

Serves 2
184 calories per serving
Takes 30 minutes

60 g (2 oz) dried risotto rice
600 ml (20 fl oz) boiling water
a few drops of vanilla essence
10 g sachet low fat hot
  chocolate drink powder
2 tablespoons low fat vanilla
  yogurt
25 g finger of fudge, sliced
  finely

This truly is the ultimate feel good food.

1 Put the rice in a non stick frying pan and start to heat. Put the boiling water in a small saucepan and keep hot on the stove over a medium heat. With a ladle, add a splash of the boiling water to the rice, stirring continuously until all the water has been absorbed. Continue to add the water, a ladleful or two at a time, stirring after each addition until the rice is tender. This will take about 20 minutes.

2 Remove the rice from the heat and stir in the vanilla essence and chocolate drink powder until combined. Spoon into bowls and top with a dollop of the yogurt and a sprinkling of the fudge. Serve immediately.

Mocha chestnut tart

Serves 10

173 calories per serving

Takes 20 minutes to prepare
+ 10 minutes cooling +
chilling, 30 minutes to cook

150 g (5½ oz) plain chocolate
(minimum 70% cocoa
solids), broken into pieces

75 g (2¾ oz) low fat spread

4 tablespoons strong black
coffee, cooled

200 g (7 oz) chestnut purée

60 g (2 oz) caster sugar

2 eggs, separated

2 egg whites

1 teaspoon cocoa powder, for
dusting

Chestnut purée is a slightly sweet, smooth paste that is found in cans, usually amongst the stuffing ingredients in supermarkets. Serve with a 60 g (2 oz) scoop of low fat ice cream per person.

1 Preheat the oven to Gas Mark 5/190°C/fan oven 170°C. Line the base of a 20 cm (8 inch) loose-bottomed tin with non stick baking parchment.

2 Place the chocolate, low fat spread and coffee in a non metallic bowl and microwave on high for 1 minute. Stir and repeat in 30 second blasts until the chocolate has melted. Mix well. Alternatively, place the bowl over a pan of simmering water, being careful that the water does not touch the bottom of the bowl, and stir gently until the chocolate has melted.

3 Beat the chestnut purée in a bowl until smooth and then beat in the sugar and egg yolks. Stir in the chocolate mixture to form a smooth paste.

4 In a clean, grease-free bowl, whisk all the egg whites until stiff peaks form. Carefully fold into the chocolate mixture. Spoon into the tin and bake for 30 minutes until firm. Cool in the tin for 10 minutes and then chill completely before serving dusted with the cocoa powder.

Key lime pie

Serves 10

235 calories per serving

Takes 15 minutes to prepare + 15 minutes chilling + cooling, 25 minutes to cook

60 g (2 oz) low fat spread

140 g (5 oz) reduced fat digestive biscuits, crushed

3 eggs, separated

405 g can skimmed sweetened condensed milk

finely grated zest and juice of 3 limes

3–4 drops green food colouring

25 g (1 oz) caster sugar

A slice of pie is a favourite American dessert. This one originates from the Florida Keys, where limes are grown.

1 Melt the low fat spread in a saucepan and add the biscuit crumbs, stirring to coat them all. Tip the coated crumbs into a 23 cm (9 inch) pie or flan dish, pressing them over the base. Chill in the fridge for about 15 minutes.

2 Preheat the oven to Gas Mark 4/180°C/fan oven 160°C.

3 Beat the egg yolks and condensed milk together and then stir in the lime zest and juice. Add a few drops of food colouring to make the mixture pale green. Pour the mixture over the prepared biscuit crumb base and bake for 15–20 minutes, until set.

4 In a clean, grease-free bowl, whisk the egg whites until stiff peaks form. Add the sugar gradually, whisking well to make stiff, glossy peaks.

5 Pile the meringue mixture on top of the lime pie, spreading it over the surface. Return it to the oven and bake for about 5–6 minutes, until the topping is golden brown.

6 Let the pie cool for about 15 minutes before serving, or you can serve it chilled.

Tip... Egg whites will not whisk successfully if there is the slightest trace of grease, including egg yolk, in the bowl or on the beaters, so make sure everything has just been washed in hot, soapy water before you begin.

Crunchie Cointreau creams

Serves 4
195 calories per serving
Takes 15 minutes + chilling

1 teaspoon Cointreau liqueur
grated zest and juice of an orange
8 sponge fingers
200 ml (7 fl oz) low fat natural yogurt
150 g (5½ oz) half fat crème fraîche
1 Crunchie bar

This is a slight twist on tiramisu – an orange version instead of the traditional coffee for those who want to try something a little different.

1 In a shallow bowl, mix together the Cointreau and orange juice. Break each sponge finger in half and dip in the orange juice mixture, allowing it to soak briefly. Place the sponge fingers in the bottom of four glasses or individual glass dishes. Pour over any remaining liquid.

2 Mix together the yogurt, crème fraîche and orange zest. Spoon the yogurt mixture over the sponge fingers.

3 Smash the Crunchie bar with a rolling pin while it is still in its wrapper. Sprinkle the crumbs on top of each dessert.

4 Chill the desserts for at least 20 minutes and up to 30 minutes before serving.

Variation... For a quick tiramisu, replace the Cointreau with Tia Maria and the orange juice with strong coffee. Sprinkle the top with 2 teaspoons of cocoa powder instead of the Crunchie bar.

Mini syrup sponge puddings

Serves 6
220 calories per serving
Takes 20 minutes to prepare,
40 minutes to cook

50 g (1¾ oz) low fat spread
50 g (1¾ oz) caster sugar
2 small eggs, beaten
100g (3½ oz) self raising flour
6 heaped teaspoons golden
syrup

These wonderful mini sponges are such a treat. Serve with 3 tablespoons of ready-made low fat custard per person.

1 Use 1 teaspoon of low fat spread to lightly grease 6 individual pudding basins with steep sides. Cream the remainder with the caster sugar until light and fluffy and then gradually beat in the eggs.

2 Fold in the flour using a metal spoon and then add 2 tablespoons of warm water to give a soft, dropping consistency.

3 Place 1 heaped teaspoon of golden syrup in the base of each mould and divide the sponge mixture between them. Cover with foil or greaseproof paper.

4 Transfer the moulds to a steamer and steam for about 40 minutes, topping up with water from time to time. Never allow the steamer to boil dry. Turn out and serve.

Variations... Substitute lemon, lime or orange marmalade for the syrup, if you prefer.

To make chocolate puddings, add 15 g (½ oz) unsweetened cocoa powder, sifting it into the mixture with the flour.

Little chocolate pots

Serves 4
180 calories per serving
Takes 20 minutes to prepare
 + chilling

2 eggs, separated
50 g (1¾ oz) caster sugar
50 g (1¾ oz) plain chocolate (minimum 70% cocoa solids), broken into pieces
150 ml (5 fl oz) 0% fat Greek yogurt

These are very light and fluffy mousses that look great served in espresso cups or little pots.

1 In a bowl, whisk the egg yolks and sugar until really thick and mousse-like.

2 Melt the chocolate in a bowl set over a pan of simmering water. Remove from the heat, allow to cool slightly and then whisk into the egg mixture. Fold the yogurt into the chocolate mixture until smooth.

3 In a clean, grease-free bowl, whisk the egg whites until stiff peaks form. Gently fold into the mixture.

4 Spoon into four little cups or pots and refrigerate until chilled and set.

Queen of puddings

Serves 4

320 calories per serving

Takes 10 minutes to prepare
+ 15 minutes soaking,
30 minutes to bake

2 teaspoons low fat spread

100 g (3½ oz) fresh white
breadcrumbs

450 ml (16 fl oz) skimmed milk

1 teaspoon vanilla extract

80 g (3 oz) caster sugar

4 eggs, separated

2 tablespoons low calorie
raspberry jam

An old-fashioned dessert that still tastes wonderful.

1 Grease a 1 litre (1¾ pint) ovenproof baking dish with
1 teaspoon of the low fat spread. Sprinkle the breadcrumbs
into the baking dish.

2 Heat the milk, remaining low fat spread and vanilla extract
until just lukewarm – take care that the mixture doesn't get too
hot. Remove from the heat and add 50 g (1¾ oz) of the sugar.
Beat in the egg yolks. Pour into the baking dish, stir into the
breadcrumbs and leave to soak for 15 minutes. Preheat the
oven to Gas Mark 4/180°C/fan oven 160°C.

3 Bake the pudding for 20–25 minutes, until set. Remove the
baking dish from the oven, cool for 5 minutes and then spread
the jam over the surface.

4 In a clean, grease-free bowl, whisk the egg whites until stiff
peaks form and then add the remaining sugar, whisking again
until stiff and glossy. Pile the meringue on top of the pudding
and return it to the oven to bake for a further 5–8 minutes, until
golden brown. Serve at once.

Tip... To make this recipe to serve 2, simply halve the
quantities.

Variation... Try replacing the raspberry jam with strawberry,
blackcurrant or apricot low calorie jam. They are all
equally delicious in this recipe.

Orchard fruit crumbles

Serves 4

192 calories per serving

Takes 20 minutes to prepare,
10–15 minutes to cook

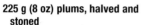

**225 g (8 oz) plums, halved and
stoned**

**225 g (8 oz) baking apples,
peeled, cored and chopped**

**40 g (1½ oz) light or dark
muscovado sugar**

25 g (1 oz) low fat spread

**75 g (2¾ oz) Jordans Crunchy
Oat Granola with Raisins and
Almonds**

To serve

**4 tablespoons low fat natural
yogurt**

**a few fresh lemon balm or
mint leaves (optional)**

*Plums and apples taste delightful in these quick and
simple crumbly fruit puddings.*

1 Put the plums, apples and sugar in a saucepan with
5 tablespoons of water. Heat and simmer gently until soft
and pulpy, about 10 minutes.

2 Preheat the oven to Gas Mark 4/180°C/fan oven 160°C.
Spoon the fruit into an ovenproof baking dish or four ramekin
dishes.

3 Melt the low fat spread in a saucepan and stir in the
granola. Sprinkle evenly over the surface of the fruit. Bake for
10–15 minutes, until crunchy and light golden brown.

4 Serve each portion with 1 tablespoon of yogurt, decorated
with lemon balm or mint leaves, if using.

Variation... If you wish, just use apples or plums, instead
of both.

Pear tart with cinnamon topping

Serves 6

116 calories per serving

Takes 10 minutes to prepare, 20 minutes to cook

calorie controlled cooking spray

4 x 15 g (½ oz) sheets filo pastry, measuring 30 x 40 cm (12 x 16 inches)

250 g (9 oz) ready-made low fat custard

2 x 410 g canned pear halves in natural juice, drained

50 g (1¾ oz) porridge oats

1 teaspoon cinnamon

1 teaspoon maple syrup

A simple tart made easy with the use of ready-made custard.

1 Preheat the oven to Gas Mark 4/180°C/fan oven 160°C.

2 Spray an 18 cm (7 inch) non stick cake or flan tin with the cooking spray. Line the tin with a sheet of filo pastry and spray with the cooking spray. Place another pastry sheet on top of the first but at a slightly different angle, so that the corners stick up. Spray again and repeat with the other two sheets of pastry so that the tin is lined. Put the tin in the oven for 2–3 minutes until slightly golden.

3 Pour the custard over the tart and arrange the pears, cut side down, on the top.

4 In a small bowl, mix together the oats, cinnamon and maple syrup. Scatter over the tart and spray again with the cooking spray. Bake for 20 minutes or until golden brown and crispy.

Tip... Keep the filo pastry under a damp tea towel as you make the tart so that it doesn't dry up.

Foolproof pineapple soufflés

Serves 4
166 calories per serving
Takes 20 minutes

calorie controlled cooking spray
75 g (2¾ oz) caster sugar
1 tablespoon cornflour
2 eggs, separated
15 g (½ oz) desiccated coconut
227 g can pineapple pieces in natural juice, drained and chopped finely

These light and spongy puddings are sure to be a huge hit.

1 Preheat the oven to Gas Mark 5/190°C/fan oven 170°C and spray four 200 ml (7 fl oz) ramekins with the cooking spray. In a bowl, whisk together half the sugar with the cornflour and egg yolks until thick and creamy.

2 In a clean, grease-free bowl, whisk the egg whites until stiff peaks form. Continuing to whisk, gradually add the remaining sugar until smooth and glossy.

3 Fold the coconut, pineapple pieces and egg whites into the egg yolk mixture until smooth. Divide equally between the ramekins and bake in the oven for 10–12 minutes until golden and risen. Serve immediately.

Tip... To ensure your soufflés rise neatly, run the tip of a knife around the edge of the mixture in each ramekin before baking in the oven.

Caramel mousse

Serves 6
135 calories per serving
Takes 45 minutes + cooling

100 g (3½ oz) caster sugar

For the mousse
juice of a lemon
3 tablespoons boiling water
15 g (½ oz) powdered gelatine
2 eggs
2 tablespoons caster sugar
6 tablespoons virtually fat free plain fromage frais
2 egg whites

It takes a little time to prepare this recipe but it is worth it as it is seductively smooth, sweet and creamy. Delicious with summer fruit or plain poached pears.

1 Make the caramel by gently heating the sugar with 300 ml (10 fl oz) of water in a saucepan. Do not stir but very occasionally pick up the pan and swirl the water around. When all the sugar has dissolved, increase the heat and bring to the boil. Boil rapidly until the mixture turns a deep, golden brown.

2 Fill the sink with a few inches of cold water and plunge the base of the saucepan into it to cool it rapidly and stop the caramel from darkening any further. Carefully add 4 tablespoons of hot water to the caramel (it may spit), stir, pour into a bowl and set aside to cool.

3 Put the lemon juice and boiling water in a bowl and sprinkle the gelatine over. Leave for a few minutes and then stir until the gelatine has dissolved.

4 Put the eggs in a bowl with the sugar and beat over a pan of simmering water for 10 minutes until the mixture thickens and will hold the trace of the whisk. Remove from the heat and allow to cool a little before adding the gelatine and caramel and stirring it all together.

5 Leave the mixture in a cool place to thicken and then fold in the fromage frais.

6 In a clean, grease-free bowl, whisk the egg whites until stiff peaks form and then fold into the mousse. Spoon into individual serving dishes and chill before serving.

Pimm's summer pudding

Serves 4
209 calories per serving
Takes 15 minutes + chilling
Ⓥ

**500 g (1 lb 2 oz) frozen
summer fruits**
50 g (1¾ oz) caster sugar
50 ml (2 fl oz) Pimm's (see Tip)
**7 medium slices bread, crusts
removed**

*Serve with a tablespoon of virtually fat free plain fromage
frais per person.*

1 Place the frozen fruits in a lidded saucepan with the caster
sugar and 100 ml (3½ fl oz) of water. Cover and cook for about
5 minutes or until the fruits have defrosted and are nice and
juicy. Remove from the heat and stir in the Pimm's.

2 Tip the fruit into a colander set over a bowl, drain for a
couple of minutes and then sit the colander back on top of
the pan.

3 Cut the bread into pieces to fit four mini pudding basins,
reserving enough bread to act as 'lids'. Dip the bread into the
warm fruit juice and use to line the pudding basins. Spoon the
fruits into the basins and top with the reserved bread 'lids',
again dipped in the fruit juice. Cover the summer puddings
with cling film, place on a plate and chill for at least 4 hours
or overnight. Strain and reserve any leftover fruit juice.

4 Unmould the summer puddings and spoon over the
reserved fruit juice to glaze.

Tip... If you don't have any Pimm's available, simply use a
total of 150 ml (5 fl oz) water instead.

Peach melba

Serves 4
141 calories per serving
Takes 11 minutes
Ⓥ

2 tablespoons cornflour
2 tablespoons caster sugar
400 ml (14 fl oz) skimmed milk
1 teaspoon vanilla extract
**411 g can peach halves in
   natural juice, drained**
**100 g (3½ oz) frozen
   raspberries**
1 tablespoon icing sugar

*A hot vanilla sauce topped with frozen raspberries creates
an amazing sensation.*

1 Dissolve the cornflour and sugar in a jug with
4 tablespoons of the milk and stir to a smooth paste.
Put the remaining milk into a saucepan and bring just to
the boil.

2 Pour the hot milk on to the cornflour mixture and stir to
combine. Return to the saucepan and gently bring to the boil
for 1 minute, stirring until thick. Stir in the vanilla extract
and then divide equally between four 250 ml (9 fl oz) dessert
bowls or glasses.

3 Reserve four peach halves and set aside. Put the
raspberries, the remaining peach halves and the icing sugar
in a food processor, or use a hand blender, and whizz until
smooth. Spoon a quarter of the raspberry sauce on top of the
vanilla sauce in each glass and then top each with a peach
half.

Tip... If you don't want to serve the dessert right away,
leave the vanilla sauce in the glasses and the raspberry
sauce in a bowl to chill in the fridge until needed.
Assemble later to serve.

Index

Other titles in the Weight Watchers Mini Series

ISBN 978-0-85720-932-0

ISBN 978-0-85720-935-1

ISBN 978-0-85720-934-4

ISBN 978-0-85720-938-2

ISBN 978-0-85720-931-3

ISBN 978-0-85720-937-5

ISBN 978-0-85720-936-8

ISBN 978-0-85720-933-7

ISBN 978-1-47111-084-9

ISBN 978-1-47111-089-4

ISBN 978-1-47111-091-7

ISBN 978-1-47111-087-0

ISBN 978-1-47111-090-0

ISBN 978-1-47111-085-6

ISBN 978-1-47111-088-7

ISBN 978-1-47111-086-3

For more details please visit www.simonandschuster.co.uk